LA'

MW01200732

continued

For volumes in the NCRLL Collection (edited by JoBeth Allen and Donna E. Alvermann) and the Practitioners Bookshelf Series
(edited by Celia Genishi and Donna E. Alvermann), as well as other titles in this series, please visit www.tcpress.com.

INCLUSIVE LITERACY TEACHING

Differentiating Approaches in Multilingual Elementary Classrooms

LORI HELMAN
CARRIE ROGERS
AMY FREDERICK
MAGGIE STRUCK

Foreword by Robert T. Jiménez

TEACHERS COLLEGE PRESS

TEACHERS COLLEGE | COLUMBIA UNIVERSITY
NEW YORK AND LONDON

Published by Teachers College Press, 1234 Amsterdam Avenue, New York, NY 10027

Library of Congress Cataloging-in-Publication Data

Names: Helman, Lori, author.
Title: Inclusive literacy teaching : differentiating approaches in multilingual
    elementary classrooms / Lori Helman, Carrie Rogers, Amy Frederick, Maggie
    Struck ; foreword by Robert Jimenez.
Description: New York, NY : Teachers College Press, [2016] | Series: Language and
    literacy series | Includes bibliographical references and index. | Description
    based on print version record and CIP data provided by publisher; resource
    not viewed.
Identifiers: LCCN 2016021432 (print) | LCCN 2016010082 (ebook) | ISBN
    9780807774915 (ebook) | ISBN 9780807757864 (pbk. : acid-free paper) |
    ISBN 9780807757871 (hardcover : alk. paper)
Subjects: LCSH: Language arts (Elementary)—United States. | Literacy—Study and
    teaching—United States. | Education, Bilingual—United States. | Multicultural
    education—United States. | Inclusive education—United States.
Classification: LCC LB1576 (print) | LCC LB1576 .H3335 2016 (ebook) | DDC
    371.9/0460973—dc23
LC record available at https://lccn.loc.gov/2016021432

ISBN 978-0-8077-5786-4 (paper)
ISBN 978-0-8077-5787-1 (hardcover)
ISBN 978-0-8077-7491-5 (ebook)

Printed on acid-free paper
Manufactured in the United States of America

23 22 21 20 19 18 17 16   8 7 6 5 4 3 2 1

This book is dedicated to
the teachers who opened up their classrooms,
the families who shared their experiences,
and, most important, the students who included us
in their educational journeys.
We have learned so much from all of you.

Contents

Foreword: Helping Linguistically Diverse Students Achieve Their Language and Literacy Potential

I wish I had read *Inclusive Literacy Teaching: Differentiating Approaches in Multilingual Elementary Classrooms* before I took my first job as a classroom teacher. Had I done so, I would have met six extraordinary children in the process of becoming bilingual (Abdirahman, Chue, Kevin, See Sing, Tong, and Ubah). These children, who are introduced at the beginning of this compelling text, provide a revealing look at the awe-inspiring diversity of what it means to be an emergent bilingual (EB) student. Had this book been available, I could have promoted more fully their transnationalism and multilingualism. The authors follow each one of their focal students across 6 years of schooling. They conclude that "the students are each vibrant human beings who bring complex personal, cultural, linguistic, and social qualities to their classroom learning experiences" (p. 3).

Those of us in the academy, as well as state and federal policymakers, have failed to adequately prepare or support teachers of EB students. Teachers have had to rely on general instructional principles or the default thinking that EB students require a slower pace and less demanding curricular demands. Another default frame for thinking about EB students is that they simply need to learn English. Both mindsets result in a lack of academic opportunity. Students learning the language of schooling while simultaneously learning content require exposure to rich, challenging curriculum and high-quality language support. This requires skillful and knowledgeable teachers.

Second-language learning is a long-term endeavor; it requires ongoing interaction with speakers of the target language and an informed teacher (Garrett, 2008). But time is a premium for EB students. To have any chance at school success they must achieve grade-level-appropriate content learning. Teachers need to become aware of the linguistic demands of the curriculum in relation to students' background knowledge (Chamot & O'Malley, 1996). Had I read this book earlier in my teaching career, I would have learned a great deal about both what I needed to teach and how best to teach it.

I also would have understood the need to more fully understand the language and schooling histories of my students and their families. I was struck by how linguistically cosmopolitan many of the six focal EB students were. Some could speak and understand languages that are currently a high priority for people in our State Department and other governmental agencies. These languages include Hmong, Somali, Arabic, and Spanish. Students' knowledge of these languages in both oral and literate forms varied, but without a doubt these young people bring a treasure trove of information into the classroom. The authors challenge readers to find out more about their students: "Knowing that a student speaks Spanish with her parents at home, plays on a local park and recreation soccer team, takes Arabic lessons at the community Mosque every Saturday, or cooks Ecuadorian meals with her grandmother on Thursday nights helps teachers understand more about who their students are and where they come from" (p. 64). Such an approach allows us to visualize these six young people as future scholars, mathematicians, scientists or artists.

One of the students, Abdirahman, provides a vivid example of what has been called translanguaging practices (García & Wei, 2014). Abdirahman uses "whatever means possible" to make sure he communicates with others. As human beings, we all have an inherent need to communicate. Careful observation of EB students as they make themselves understood reveals their creativity and intelligence rather than any supposed linguistic shortcomings.

Finally, had I read this book much sooner, I would have better been able to understand and communicate with the parents of my students. Echoing attitudes reported in other research studies, parents of the six focal students want the best for their children, but they go about this work using what they know and believe about the world. Tong's father tells his son, "If you don't know how to read, just copy the words down." This advice would make perfect sense in other parts of the world. These authors learned that the parents "did not understand how grading works, how standards are set, what standards their children need to achieve, what tests are given and what those test scores mean, attendance procedures, or other district policies" (p. 87). Who better to explain it to them than their children's teachers?

EB students deserve excellent content and language instruction. Resources such as *Inclusive Literacy Teaching* support the professional learning of EB teachers in a respectful and practical manner.

—Robert T. Jiménez
Vanderbilt University

REFERENCES

Chamot, A. U., & O'Malley, J. M. (1996). The cognitive academic language learning approach: A model for linguistically diverse classrooms. *Elementary School
Journal (96)3, 259–273.*

García, O., & Wei, L. (2014). *Translanguaging: Language, bilingualism and education.* New York, NY: Palgrave MacMillan.

Garrett, N. (2008). What does it take to learn a language well? *The 5-minute
linguist* [Audio podcast]. Retrieved from: itunes.apple.com/us/itunes-u
/the-five-minute-linguist/id452255394?mt=10

Acknowledgments

We would like to acknowledge the families, the students, and the teachers who took time to meet with us—in classrooms, living rooms, neighborhood cafes, and public libraries. This book wouldn't exist without your stories. Thank you to the administrators of the five schools we worked with who granted us permission to be participant observers alongside the students and teachers in this endeavor. Many thanks go to district staff, including the bilingual interpreters and translators who helped us communicate with families, as well as the ELL personnel who helped us forge the initial connections. Thank you to the multiple public and school librarians who let us use library space for interviews with both students and families. Thanks to the Minnesota Center for Reading Research staff—specifically, office managers Meaghan and Brad who helped with technical tasks related to data and formatting. This project began thanks to a grant-in-aid from the Graduate School at the University of Minnesota. Without this funding for a graduate assistant, such comprehensive data collection would not have been possible.

We appreciate the efforts of Emily Spangler, Teachers College Press acquisitions editor, in shepherding this project and supporting us. We also thank the series editors, Dorothy S. Strickland, Celia Genishi, and Donna E. Alvermann, for including our book in their important collection. Many thanks to our production editor John Bylander for his conscientious support. We are indebted to the thoughtful reviewers of our initial chapters, who helped us make this book more clear and practical for current and future teachers.

We also thank those who helped us think more deeply about this work: scholars who responded to our papers at conferences, and colleagues and students at the University of Minnesota. In particular we want to thank Martha Bigelow and Bic Ngo, who helped us conceptualize our work and relationships with the immigrant families involved.

Finally, we send a special thank you out to our own families for their support throughout this process, in particular to our partners, who made dinner, took the kid to his lesson, and let us hole up and work even when they wanted to go out and have fun: Michael, Elizabeth, Mike, and Donald. And thanks to Harold for being a good sport.

INCLUSIVE LITERACY TEACHING

CHAPTER 1

Language and Literacy Learning in Diverse Classrooms

We're glad you've chosen to investigate *Inclusive Literacy Teaching: Differentiating Approaches in Multilingual Elementary Classrooms*, a book that provides guidance on classroom-level differentiation and support for teachers by examining the concrete examples of a group of students who came from three different language backgrounds and learned English during their elementary school years. We have written this book for current and future teachers, teacher educators, and educational leaders who are working to ensure that all students have greater opportunities to succeed in their general education classrooms. In this book we shine a light on teaching and learning in multilingual settings where predominantly monolingual English-speaking teachers work with students from many linguistic and cultural backgrounds. These complex and inclusive learning communities are becoming the norm in elementary classrooms across the United States.

As you read this book you will engage with issues that arise in the language and literacy development of six diverse students with whom the authors worked from 1st through 6th grade. We combine our school observations with the research literature to present both a "big picture" and an "up-close and personal" look at the successes, obstacles, and developmental nuances and commonalities for students learning to read and write in a new language in inclusive classrooms. As former teachers and current teacher educators, we work to capture the elementary students' experiences for you as the reader and educator. We share our own reactions to a number of instructional situations while also encouraging your reflections.

This book consists of an overview chapter and six topic-area chapters that each introduce a complex dilemma in language and literacy instruction for linguistically diverse students in elementary classrooms. These dilemmas emerged from the data and artifacts we collected of student learning. We assessed students using formal and informal measures of their language and literacy growth, conducted multiple classroom observations each year, and interviewed parents and teachers. In the Appendix we describe our multiple-case-study research for those who are interested in more details.

A WORD ABOUT THE LANGUAGE WE USE

Throughout this book we use a variety of terms to describe the students with whom we work, such as *emergent bilingual* or *multilingual student*. Nuances exist across these labels, so we want to take a moment to explain our thinking right from the start. Table 1.1 outlines some of the terms you will find that depict the experiences and backgrounds of students. While many of these descriptors overlap in meaning, there are fine distinctions that we considered when using the terms.

In this book we talk in depth about language, culture, and learning, and these concepts necessitate some technical vocabulary. For this reason, we have included a glossary with key terms that are used. The first time we use a word that is in the glossary, you will see it in boldface.

Table 1.1. Language Descriptors

Descriptor	A Student Who . . .
Emergent Bilingual	. . . brings a non-English home language to school and learns English there. An emergent bilingual is gaining English proficiency along with home language proficiency, thereby becoming bilingual.
Linguistically Diverse Student	. . . brings a home language other than standardized academic English to school. Linguistically diverse students may speak English as a first language; however, it may be a variation of English that is different from the language used in schooling (e.g., African American English or Spanish-influenced English).
Transnational Student (or Family)	. . . has ties across national borders either because the family immigrated to the United States or because there is an ongoing family relationship with people or places in other countries. These connections also may take shape in relationships in the United States with fellow immigrants from specific geographical regions.
English Learner or **English Language Learner**	. . . is in the process of learning English as a new language. We make an effort to avoid this term because it positions the student as "lacking" in ability, rather than highlighting that he or she is becoming bilingual. We employ the descriptor when referencing the research literature and national and local programs that use the term.
Multilingual Student	. . . operates in various languages or dialects throughout his or her life in and out of school. Students use more than one language to interact with friends, family, church members, and/or the community, and to transition across these discourse communities.

MEET THE STUDENTS

Throughout this book we zoom in and out of the unique stories of six multilingual students to learn from their challenges and successes. We share the data we collected and think out loud about what the students' experiences imply for learning to be an effective teacher of linguistically diverse students. We put background notes about the students in an easy-to-access location in this introductory chapter in case you want to reference them as you read more about the individual students in the topic-area chapters. All of the students we describe lived in the same midwestern city and began school at Randolph Elementary (pseudonym).

We use pseudonyms for the students, but other than that, we report their backgrounds and experiences as they were. We describe the students using identity markers of race, social class, and gender, thus taking the multiplicity and complexity of culture and identity and simplifying it into a series of labels. In reality these labels cannot capture the fluid, complex, and nuanced lives and experiences of the real students and teachers we observed. It is important to remember that these categories are never fixed and in using these identity markers care should be taken to not essentialize or stereotype people based on them.

The students are all vibrant human beings who bring complex personal, cultural, linguistic, and social qualities to their classroom learning experiences. It was a great joy for us to learn from their elementary literacy journeys, and we know they are proud that their experiences will help you as teachers to better meet the needs of multilingual students in your classrooms as well.

Abdirahman

Abdirahman, a confident and active Somali-speaking student who dynamically tackled all of the academic tasks sent his way.

Abdirahman arrived in the United States from Kenya in the middle of his kindergarten year. His enrollment at the urban public school near his house marked his first formal schooling experience. Abdirahman lived with his mother and six brothers. His mother spoke Somali to her children and taught them the Koran in Arabic at home, so they learned to read and write Arabic. The children in Abdirahman's family frequently use English when talking to one another or watching TV. Abdirahman's mother learned to speak English after coming to the United States but made a point of speaking Somali with her children, as well as Arabic, because she felt it was important for them to understand their home culture. Equally important to her was that her children learn English and do well in school in the United States.

Over the course of Abdirahman's elementary years, his mother took an active role in supporting him in his English literacy and language education—by taking him to the library, finding tutors, buying extra books for the summer, and, during particular years, working at his charter school.

Chue

Chue, a peer-focused, Hmong-speaking boy who had difficulty learning academic skills in English.

Chue belongs to a Hmong family that emigrated from Laos by way of a Thai refugee camp and spoke Hmong in the home. Chue's family arrived in the United States prior to his entering kindergarten. Chue is the youngest of nine brothers and sisters, and he followed in their footsteps at the same elementary school. At home, the family spoke mainly Hmong. His father attended school in Thailand and learned to read and write in Hmong. In an early interview, Chue's mother shared that her eldest son spoke English to her "all the time," and the younger kids used both languages at home.

Six years later, as Chue was about to enter middle school, his mother indicated that he used English very little around the home, and she was concerned that he might not be learning enough English to be successful. She encouraged the use and development of his Hmong language so that he could understand his culture, but she also wanted him to be successful in English.

Kevin

Kevin, a good-humored, Spanish-speaking boy who showed dramatic language and literacy growth throughout his elementary years.

Kevin's family came to this large midwestern city in the United States from Mexico when he was 6 years old, shortly before beginning 1st grade. He and his mother joined other family members who had immigrated previously and moved into a cooperative household setting. Kevin is an only child, but in his household there were many adults and a few children. His grandmother cared for him when his mother was at work. Kevin spoke primarily Spanish in the home.

Kevin attended preschool/kindergarten for 2 years in Mexico, where he began to learn to read in Spanish, before coming to the United States. His mother worked with him at home to continue his Spanish literacy development.

See Sing

See Sing, a thoughtful Hmong-speaking girl who hovered below the radar of her teachers' attention throughout her elementary career.

See Sing and her family came to a large midwestern city in the United States when she was 4 years old. They were members of the Hmong community who had lived as refugees in temporary camps in Thailand prior to their immigration.

There are five children in See Sing's family ranging from 1 year old to 8 years old. She is the second oldest. See Sing attended Head Start when she arrived in the United States and then began kindergarten at a public elementary school with a special program for new immigrants. At home, her father usually helped her with her homework. He also read to her and taught her some Hmong. Other times, her mother's sister came to help. At home, See Sing spoke mostly Hmong but sometimes spoke English with her older sister.

Tong

Tong, a kind and relationship-centered, Hmong-speaking boy who experienced language challenges that made learning tasks at school difficult for him.

Tong's family came to a large midwestern city in the United States about 5 years before he was born. Like See Sing's family, Tong's was part of the Hmong community and had lived as refugees in temporary camps in Thailand prior to immigrating. There are five children in the family ranging from 2 years old to 18 years old. Tong is the second youngest. Tong attended Head Start and then began kindergarten at a public elementary school with a special program for new immigrants. At home, Tong spoke mainly Hmong with his parents, siblings, and friends. He watched English television and shared the English books he brought home from school.

Ubah

Ubah, an inquisitive Somali-speaking girl who made consistent progress at school in part because of her parents' laser-like attention to the rigor of her classroom experiences.

Ubah was born in the United States and attended Head Start classes prior to her family returning to Nairobi, Kenya. In Nairobi, she attended an English-speaking school for kindergarten. Ubah returned to Randolph Elementary in 1st grade. There are three children in her family; she has an older brother and a younger sister. Her father was licensed to practice medicine in Kenya and often traveled there for work. He was away for extended periods of time.

Ubah's mother and father spoke some English but used Somali with their children. Both parents worked with their children to help them know the Somali language. Her mother taught her Somali numbers and the alphabet as well as other literacy skills.

NO SIMPLE PATH TO ACQUIRING "SCHOOL" LITERACY

It is our goal in this first chapter to construct a foundation for the content in future chapters, showing the integral connection between language and literacy development, and the factors that influence literacy learning for multilingual students. We begin by sharing a vignette and observations of See Sing at the beginning of 1st grade. She had attended a school-based preschool before entering kindergarten at this public school, which housed a special program for emergent bilinguals called **Language Academy**. She spent part of her day in a classroom with teachers who were specially trained to teach English and literacy skills, and part of her day in a mainstream 1st-grade classroom.

> In a bustling 1st- and 2nd-grade classroom at Randolph Elementary in a large midwestern city, students are busy reading to volunteers, reading alone, or working in small groups with their teacher. See Sing, an immigrant student from a Hmong family, is practicing sounding out simple words with a small group of English learners under her teacher's guidance. The word is *fin* and the teacher helps the students sound it out: /f/ /i/ /n/.
> *Teacher:* What is a fin?
> *See Sing:* Fin is a fish.
> *Teacher:* Something with a fish? Fin is part of a fish.
>
> *As See Sing sounds out other words along with the teacher, they come to the word* kit.
>
> *Teacher:* What is kit?
> *See Sing:* Kit . . . kitten . . . like cute.

In this short classroom excerpt, we see a very common example of the challenge of literacy teaching and learning with **emergent bilinguals**, students who speak one language at home and learn English at school. The teacher is working on a skill that is important to **decoding** print— sounding out phonetically regular words such as *fin*. Clearly, this is an essential skill that will help 1st-graders gain access to written texts. Even as teacher and student work together to apply this learning, however, it is evident that the path will be complex. There may be tensions between when it is best to stop and clarify confusions or vocabulary and when it is best to keep presenting the material. By not clarifying See Sing's confusion about what *fin* or *kit* means, the teacher risks reinforcing these conceptual misunderstandings. In order to be successful, See Sing will need to both decode phonetically regular short vowel words and know what these words mean. This type of instruction requires professional knowledge and teacher responsiveness.

The embroidered fabric in Figure 1.1 is a Hmong "story cloth"—or *paj ntaub* (pronounced "pan dow"). Intricate, colorful needlework has been a part of the Hmong culture for centuries, but in the past 30 years story cloths have emerged as a way for the Hmong to record and keep their stories alive (Lee & Low Books, 2013). Each cloth created tells a story of Hmong culture. See Sing's family story spanned the traditional practices of the Hmong people as reflected in the story cloth, and extended to new settings and evolving traditions as her family moved from the countryside into refugee camps, and then again when they immigrated to the United States.

Figure 1.1. Story Cloth

"A Great Little Decoder"

See Sing began 1st grade with strong early literacy skills in phonemic aware-ness, phonics, and developmental spelling. Her English oral language as-sessment results, however, put her in the least proficient category, labeling her "non-English speaking." By 2nd grade, her teacher described her as "a great little decoder," although she worried about See Sing's comprehension of English. Developing reading proficiency is a process of integrating both code-based skills such as phonics and word recognition, and meaning-based skills such as vocabulary and comprehension (Lesaux & Marietta, 2012). See Sing was succeeding in the code-based area but was just beginning to acquire the extensive vocabulary she would need for deep comprehension of texts. See Chapter 3 for a more extensive discussion of the role of **academic language**—the language of schooling—in reading comprehension.

Across the grade levels, See Sing maintained a learning trajectory that approached, but did not meet, benchmark standards in reading. She expe-rienced the greatest reading improvement in 2nd grade, when her scores showed growth from a kindergarten to a 2nd-grade reading level. During most other years, See Sing hovered slightly below the target grade-level score, and she plateaued at a 3rd-grade reading level for several years. See Sing frequently lost ground over the summer months and started off the new school year behind where she had been the previous spring. By the end of 6th grade, See Sing's standardized reading results were 16 points lower (201 out of 217) than the average score of 6th-graders nationwide who took the same assessment (Northwest Evaluation Association, 2011). This put her at the 15th percentile for her norm group.

See Sing was always quiet and well-behaved at school, and her teachers described her as "a delight," "hardworking," and "motivated." Her 6th-grade teacher said, "She has a strong work ethic. She thinks it is important to be educated and be in school. I see that in her behavior all the time, in how she takes responsibility for her homework, and all the things she does at the beginning of independent reading." Although a few teachers men-tioned their concern about her vocabulary needs and reluctance to speak up in class, in general she operated "under the radar" of teachers' concerns. Perhaps for this reason, or because there were many other students who were performing below her on grade-level benchmarks, See Sing did not receive the extra help she needed to catch up. In Chapter 6, we will take a closer look at the curriculum continuity that See Sing experienced, and in the final chapter will reflect on the instructional opportunities that could have helped See Sing in her elementary school years. Figure 1.2 shows a passage that See Sing wrote at the end of 6th grade that touchingly describes a friend who moved away when the two girls were in kindergarten. In this passage we see her thoughtfulness and appreciation for social relationships. We also see her use of basic vocabulary and some continued confusion with

Figure 1.2. See Sing's 6th-Grade Story

I remember in kindgarten, playing with my friends . . . and there was a girl that I know, she and I became friends, the week pass by she said that she have to move to a different school. Me, and my other friend doesn't want her to move at all, because she's a nice girl, kind, sweet, friendly, but she have to move, then we spend a lot of times w/her before we dont get to see her anymore. then next day I came to school my friend say "I miss her already". We didn't see her sever since she move in kindgarten.

English spelling, grammar, and syntax. Chapter 2 discusses in more depth the cross-linguistic challenges that students may have when their home language is dissimilar from the language of schooling.

What My Heart Wishes

In an interview with See Sing's family after she had finished 6th grade, her parents described their perceptions of how she had progressed in learning to read and write in elementary school. Her father shared:

> If you think about it, she is very good at English. She comes home from school and does her reading and writing. Based on my thinking, I don't know what she does at school. I think she does well. We just recently came and we don't understand English well, and can't read and write it. So, I'm not sure how well she is doing at school, but at home she does her homework. When we go meet the teachers at school they say she seems to be doing well. It also seems that she is shy to speak.

Over the years the family has attended parent conferences regularly, and the teachers told them that See Sing was "doing well." Although See Sing's parents did not speak a lot of English, they saw themselves as having an important role in making sure that their daughter studied hard. When she couldn't figure out what to do in her homework, they called in a member of their extended family to help her. See Sing's mother stated, "I tell [her] to study hard because I want children who listen well and work hard and study. Because we recently came and we can't go to school, so I want them to do what my heart wishes for them." In Chapter 4 we delve into the importance of home–school connections and building on those relationships at school.

For her part, See Sing, in reflecting on her literacy journey in elementary school, recalled, "Well, it was kind of hard in elementary but later it got easier." She says that, beginning in 4th grade, her English was better and she could comprehend more. She noted two special teachers who were able to help her a lot because they "give us specific directions and help us to understand."

See Sing's experiences highlight the powerful connections between language and literacy development. Through her experiences, and those of the other students we observed, we witnessed the successes, challenges, and individual highlights for students as they progressed on the path to "school" literacy. Each individual taught us about what can go wrong or right for students in elementary classrooms. Renowned photographer Diane Arbus, whose iconic photographs highlighted human traits that extended beyond her individual subjects, said, "The more specific you are, the more general it'll be" (Israel & Arbus, 2011). It is impossible to understand English learners' paths to literacy learning as a conglomerate or as a generic experience; rather, it is through a variety of specific, individual examples that teachers may develop a deeper knowledge of students' challenges and successes.

WHAT DOES LITERACY PROFICIENCY MEAN?

Becoming literate, or having competence in literacy, can mean very different things depending on the task, context, participants, and purpose involved (Kalantzis, Cope, & Harvey, 2003). In elementary school, literacy success often is defined by progress through a series of reading and writing standards that are benchmarked for each grade level, such as understanding the main idea of a text or applying grade-level phonics. Literacy also can be seen as a competence in certain socially validated activities, such as reading text for personal enjoyment or to accomplish a task (Knoblauch, 1990). Literacy may be defined as the ability to write a cohesive narrative or demonstrate understanding of essential content knowledge. From the perspective of multilingual families, being able to use two or more languages in a variety of social and academic settings may be essential to being a literate person (Bailey & Osipova, 2015).

Literacy extends far beyond the ability to read and write basic texts. Students are expected to read complex texts with accuracy, fluency, and comprehension. They are called upon to produce and publish informative and creative writing. Literacy competency also includes drawing information from print and digital sources and presenting this knowledge (National Governors Association Center for Best Practices & Council of Chief State School Officers [NGA & CCSO], 2010).

What does literacy proficiency mean for See Sing? As an adolescent, she enjoys keeping a journal and texting with her friends. She is certainly using multiple literacies in purposeful ways in her daily life. See Sing's mother hopes that her daughter will be a nurse and bring bilingualism to her career. To be a proficient nurse, she will need many literacy skills, including comprehending and applying the latest developments in patient care, and communicating in writing and through technology (American Association of Colleges of Nursing, 2008). See Sing's language arts skills at the end of 6th grade would need to be significantly enhanced in secondary school for her to be able to enter a nursing program and acquire the type of specialized literacy skills needed in the profession.

THE WEAVE OF LANGUAGE AND LITERACY

For all students, the path to academic literacy learning involves the acquisition of print-based skills that are foundational to reading and writing, such as learning the alphabetic principle; identifying sounds in words and representing them with letters; and fluently decoding and understanding words, sentences, and cohesive texts. Native English speakers who have deep knowledge of the words and syntactical structures of their home language may obfuscate the deep-seated principle that language underlies all of these important foundational skills. Language knowledge may be taken for granted and be invisible in classrooms composed only of native English-speaking students with strong language experiences. In more-diverse classrooms with students who bring other home languages to school or fewer experiences with standardized academic English, however, the language–literacy relationship is obvious in every facet of teaching and learning (Genishi & Dyson, 2009). For example, students will find it much easier to match letters to speech sounds when the oral language they know and the writing system they are learning are the same. Otherwise, issues of distinguishing the sounds across languages (e.g., *sh/ch, b/p, l/r*) or even understanding what word is being spoken may be difficult. Students who know many words in English will begin more easily to categorize words by their beginning sounds, for example, being able to identify that *top, tell, table*, and *tiger* all begin with the /t/ sound. And, of course, decoding words and sentences does not ensure that emergent bilinguals understand what they are reading; this comprehension is based on knowledge of the vocabulary and academic language structures, in addition to the background knowledge of each student.

At the beginning of this chapter we presented a brief vignette involving See Sing as a 1st-grader learning phonics. The teacher's basic questions point out that See Sing did not understand what the words *fin* and *kit* meant. This example highlights the tenet that even seemingly simple literacy lessons cannot be isolated from the language that students possess. More than a year later, in late 2nd grade, we observed See Sing working on a comprehension activity with a partner in her classroom. See Sing flipped through the book *Stellaluna* (Cannon, 2008) but did not seem to find what she was looking for. The teacher approached her and asked, "What does the word *clumsy* mean?" See Sing looked at her without responding. The teacher asked another student to help her, and this student brought the educational assistant into the discussion. The assistant acted out *clumsy* as someone tripping. See Sing wrote on her worksheet, "Stellaluna clumsy on the branch and that mean you trit. Then Stellaluna trit on a tree." When asked to read her writing, See Sing read trit as "trip." Once again, a basic classroom activity demonstrates the tight relationship between language and literacy. See Sing could not fully understand the story or do her comprehension activity when she didn't know the meaning of particular words, or even *which* words in the story were the most important ones to attend to.

Every learning event in an elementary classroom with emergent bilinguals is an opportunity to build language, whether that learning is at the word level (content or general academic vocabulary) or at the sentence or paragraph level. Chapter 3 focuses on the importance of academic language development and how teachers can explicitly support it in the classroom. In the examples from See Sing's classroom experiences presented above, it is clear that listening carefully to what students are saying, or looking carefully at what they are writing, gives the teacher important information to set language goals. Literacy instruction separated from language engagement creates a dead-end pathway, rather than a thoroughfare to new knowledge.

OVERVIEW OF FACTORS INFLUENCING LITERACY LEARNING

Developing reading and writing capabilities in a new language involves a complex interweaving of related yet distinct threads. These various components can be conceptualized within linguistic, psychological, sociocultural, and educational frameworks (Helman, 2009). Individual learners bring with them to school a home language with sounds, syntax, vocabulary, and communication patterns that they used in early interactions. Individuals also bring thinking skills, varying levels of literacy skills in a home language, inquisitiveness, motivation, cultural ways of being, family support, and so much more. Table 1.2 outlines four main factors that interact for multilingual students as they learn to read and write in English. These factors include the assets students bring to the learning environment—such as their language and cultural backgrounds—and also how the school setting supports or doesn't support their learning of unfamiliar material. For example, multilingual students do better when they have well-prepared teachers who use evidence-based instructional practices, engage families and communities, and provide opportunities to learn with high-quality materials (Samson & Collins, 2012; Shatz & Wilkinson, 2010).

Table 1.2. Factors That Influence Emergent Bilinguals' Literacy Development

Factor	An Example from See Sing's Experience
LINGUISTIC ELEMENTS	
Phonology: How similar are the sound systems of the student's home language and English? The more similar they are, the easier it will be to learn the new language.	The Hmong and English sound systems are quite different, and this often stymied See Sing's attempts to correctly represent sounds in words, especially consonant endings that are not used in Hmong.
Syntax: In what ways are the grammar and sentence structures different between the student's home language and English? Significant differences can affect students' ability to predict upcoming words in texts or to create grammatically correct sentences in speaking or writing.	At different grade levels See Sing demonstrated confusion with English sentence structures (e.g., substituting READ for *reading*) or using incorrect verb tenses (e.g., using MAKE for *made*).
Vocabulary: How many and what kinds of words does the student know in English? Knowing more words, especially the academic words used in school texts, will facilitate learning alphabetic skills, fluency, comprehension, and writing development. Latinate languages that have many **cognates** with English will provide greater clues to new vocabulary.	Hmong and English do not share cognates, although some English words have been incorporated into Hmong. An emerging vocabulary constrained See Sing's progress at each step in her reading and writing development.
Pragmatics: How is the student's home language used in social and academic interactions in ways that are similar to or different from English? Being familiar with guidelines such as turn-taking and listening, eye contact, proximity, and so on, helps students to feel competent in language interactions in English.	See Sing was reserved in her interactions and perceived as well-behaved and attentive by her teachers. These "polite behaviors" may overlap with pragmatics in the Hmong community for gender roles (a quiet, attentive demeanor in women). Nonetheless, the subdued ways of being perhaps did not contribute to See Sing's linguistic engagement in class.
PSYCHOLOGICAL ELEMENTS	
Cognitive strengths: What "in the head" resources does the student bring, such as working memory, problem solving, or **metalinguistic** insights? These assets will support students in learning to read in an unfamiliar language.	We saw many strengths in our observations of See Sing, including her alertness to classroom happenings and her thoughtful, reflective nature.
Literacy skills: Does the student have reading or writing capabilities in a language other than English? Many of these literate practices will transfer to learning about the writing system of English and an understanding of generic reading processes.	See Sing did not have the opportunity to acquire literacy skills from her home language, nor did she have many models of Hmong readers and writers at home, as the language is used primarily to communicate orally.

Table 1.2. Factors That Influence Emergent Bilinguals' Literacy Development (continued)

Factor	An Example from See Sing's Experience
Affective and personal strengths: What individual resources does the student bring to learning the new language? A high or low level of motivation? A willingness to use the new language prior to mastery? A general inquisitiveness about languages? These and many other personal factors may influence the rate and depth of new language and literacy acquisition.	See Sing was shy and focused on her peer group of Hmong-speaking girls. Because of her quietness, she may have stayed under the radar of her teachers. This also may have limited her practice in using oral English.

SOCIOCULTURAL ELEMENTS

Cultural values: What norms for interacting or other "ways of being" do students bring to the classroom related to language and literacy learning? Patterns in the home for sharing information orally or in written form; culturally based narrative styles; tendencies to work collaboratively or independently; or preferred ways of interacting with school personnel all influence the student's participation in literacy-learning events in the classroom.	See Sing brought family values that honor the importance of schooling and respect for teachers. At home, interactions were primarily collaborative and oral. School settings that were focused on individualism, competition, and product completion may have seemed quite different from her home experiences.
Funds of knowledge: What assets do students bring to the classroom from their homes and communities? Students bring background experiences, languages, communicative competence, interests, histories, family support, and so much more. These strengths help students to understand the academic world from their own perspective and make the most of it.	See Sing's family deeply valued her schooling opportunities, in large part because they had not had these experiences themselves. Her parents encouraged her to maintain the Hmong language and her culture even as she learned English and school procedures. In the home See Sing was expected to share responsibility for household duties and caring for family members. With the significant population of Hmong students at See Sing's school, many of her teachers became informed about cultural practices that they could connect to school experiences.
Language prestige: To what extent is the student's home language esteemed at school, and is the student encouraged to model and be proud of bilingual skills? Students who aim for bilingualism can explicitly use their home language skills at school to negotiate language and literacy development in English.	English was clearly the prestige language at school; however, Hmong students had opportunities to speak with peers in their home language and get clarifying explanations related to content from educational assistants. While teachers supported students' use of Hmong in the classroom or on the playground, no formal structure was created to develop bilingualism or biliteracy.

Use of English: What opportunities do students have to practice oral and written English in and out of school? If students interact in limited ways in class, and do not practice English at home or in their neighborhoods, their language proficiency may take longer to develop, and that may impact their literacy progress as well.

See Sing was in specially designed language support classrooms throughout elementary school; however, because of her shyness, she did not often speak up. Out of school she used primarily the Hmong language, although she was exposed to English in the community and through media.

TEACHING AND LEARNING ELEMENTS

Teaching approaches: What evidence-based practices do teachers use in the classroom to support English learners' literacy development? Teaching matters, and students who experience quality literacy instruction that is tailored specifically to their strengths and needs likely will experience greater success.

See Sing experienced a range of teachers and teaching approaches across elementary school, many of which were tailored to improving English learners' oral language and literacy skills. She was served by English language learner (ELL) specialists throughout the elementary years.

Opportunities to learn: Do English learners experience the grade-level content and instructional strategies in sufficient depth and with equal access as compared with their native English-speaking peers? Or are they receiving diluted or scaled-back curricula, poor instructional materials, and/or underprepared teachers? If students are underserved at school, they will be unlikely to reach high-level learning goals.

See Sing experienced a collaborative-teaching model that paired a classroom teacher and ELL specialist in order to provide grade-level curriculum as well as extra language support. Across the years, services varied from co-teaching to small-group, pull-out sessions. Because there was a continual influx of new immigrants at See Sing's school, the curricula may have been scaled back so they would be accessible to emergent students. Compared with other students in the state, she was not adequately meeting standards.

Structures and programs: What school and classroom structures are in place to support the participation and engagement of multilingual students and their families? Schoolwide procedures for homework, translated parent newsletters, a welcoming multilingual environment, and graphic support for behavior expectations and academic routines are examples of systemic methods that invite students to be successful at school.

There was some consistency in schoolwide programs at See Sing's school, and evidence of encouraging families to be involved. For example, the school employed a Hmong interpreter and community liaisons, and sent out notices translated into the Hmong language. See Sing's family attended conferences but did not feel that they understood what happened at school very well.

Teacher professional development: What opportunities do instructional personnel (e.g., classroom teachers, educational assistants, and specialists) have to learn about, try out, and refine their capabilities for working with emergent bilinguals in language and literacy development? Collaborative professional development that examines student achievement data in relation to state standards in each school's particular context will be the most helpful for ensuring that instruction is on track for emergent bilinguals.

Grade-level teachers and English language development (ELD) specialists at See Sing's school experienced professional learning opportunities relating to language development, differentiated instruction, and balanced literacy assessment and instruction. Staff functioned as teams to co-plan and analyze the needs of the students with whom they worked.

MULTILINGUAL SCHOOLS AND CLASSROOMS

Teachers in elementary classrooms have students who bring a range of language experiences, academic skills, and interests with them. Some students, such as See Sing, are learning to read and write for the first time as they learn to speak English. The number of emergent bilinguals and the variety of home languages they speak are increasing across the United States, and most communities are finding the need to make sure that all of their teachers are prepared to teach linguistically diverse students within the classroom. If students are not prepared to access the curriculum in secondary school, they are more likely to disengage and potentially drop out of school. It is crucial that educators find ways to differentiate instruction to enhance all students' academic achievement.

One need look no further than current teacher evaluation standards to see that capable teachers are expected to "address the specific needs of English learners" (California Commission on Teacher Credentialing, 2009, p. 14), create "opportunities for students to learn, practice, and master in their content" (Council of Chief State School Officers, 2011, p. 13), and provide "explicit instruction in and accommodations for their oral language development" (National Board for Professional Teaching Standards, 2012, p. 68). These proficiencies are important for both experienced and novice teachers, and must be integrated into teacher preparation programs as well as ongoing professional learning opportunities (Lenski, Mack, & Brown, 2008). Someone who is not able to understand how language has an impact on learning or is unable to provide tailored instruction to students no longer can be considered an effective teacher. Current and future teachers need to have a repertoire of effective practices to make the most of their "multilingual classroom ecologies" (Creese & Martin, 2003).

Essential Dilemma: What happens if educators do not take into account students' languages, cultures, and background experiences as they teach reading and writing?

What specific tools do teachers need in order to identify how to best serve their multilingual students? Throughout this book we present a number of dispositions and actions teachers can take, and the tools they will need to apply them. For example, in Chapters 2 and 4 you will learn about how educators must have a deep understanding of the resources that students bring with them to the classroom, so that these can be built upon (Moll & González, 1994). In Chapter 3 you will explore how educators need to be able to put their knowledge of the threaded relationship between language and literacy development into practice in the lessons they teach (Scarborough, 2001). Key to this process is the ability to make formative assessments in the moment—an idea discussed throughout this book—to ensure that students understand their classroom learning experiences (Heritage, 2013).

One recent approach to tailoring instruction for emergent bilinguals has been to set up collaborative teaching or planning among classroom teachers and ELL specialists (Dove & Honigsfeld, 2010), and this will be addressed in Chapter 6. Getting knowledgeable professionals together to reflect on data and plan instruction is an important first step (Costello, 1987; Friend, 2008). It can provide a gateway for sharing expertise and reflecting more deeply, as well as surfacing questions that need to be addressed.

Recently we asked classroom teachers and ELL specialists what they needed to know to be better teachers of their students. Classroom teachers had many specific questions about reading comprehension and students' vocabulary knowledge. They wanted information about how to know the difference between a language development issue and a learning problem. They wondered how they might learn about language standards and collaborate with ELL specialists. When asked about their concerns and interests, ELL support teachers were eager to interact more with mainstream teachers. They wanted to work together to elucidate the various challenges and opportunities for ensuring the success of emergent bilinguals.

Whether we consider teacher preparation and evaluation standards, district achievement expectations for each student, or voices from practitioners in elementary classrooms, there is a consensus concerning the need to equip teachers with the knowledge and skills to tailor instruction for multilingual and potentially **transnational** students. Without teachers who can deliver this differentiated instruction, students who are learning English at school will not be able to call upon their cultural and linguistic strengths as they access the important curriculum needed for school and career success.

Although our case study student in this chapter, See Sing, represents only one possible experience for multilingual students, she is a realistic example of what the language- and literacy-learning process could look like for an individual student who comes to school with a home language and background experiences that are different from what educational personnel judge to be foundational. In the second column of Table 1.2 we noted examples of how See Sing's experience reflected the factors involved in literacy learning at school. These examples are not meant to be exhaustive; rather, we hope to elucidate some of the complexities that arose in her particular literacy journey.

SUMMARIZING LEARNING AND LOOKING AHEAD

Observing See Sing's journey through the elementary school years reinforced and problematized many of the ideas we held about what literacy development involves, as well as what good literacy and language instruction encompasses for students learning English. In the topic-area chapters that follow we use longitudinal data from See Sing and five other students to discuss, examine, clarify, and question the ways that factors in and outside of school contributed to their language and literacy learning. We believe that by learning about and reflecting upon students' specific literacy experiences, educators will be better prepared to thoughtfully tackle the many teaching opportunities that arise in their daily practice.

In Chapter 2 we focus on what students bring to school and what they encounter there that is different or unknown to them. In this chapter we consider the dilemma: What if students' background knowledge does not match school expectations?

In Chapter 3 we highlight the students' difficulties in developing the academic language necessary to understand disciplinary and procedural content at school. The dilemma we present is: Language learning takes time, yet "waiting for language" puts students further and further behind in content learning.

In Chapter 4 we describe the ways that students become excited and engaged at school, and what teachers do to help this happen. The dilemma for this chapter is: How do you build relationships with students and their families when you don't speak their home language or come from the same cultural or discourse communities that they do?

Chapter 5 focuses on what educators can do to create closer connections between families and schools, with the goal of increasing the academic success of their students. The chapter's essential dilemma is: How can school personnel break through ingrained practices to create structures that are more culturally and linguistically responsive to the lives of students' families?

In Chapter 6 we delve into the elementary experiences of each of the focus students. The dilemma we investigate centers on how the year-by-year cycle of schools may lead to fragmented experiences for students, rather than a connected and cohesive program.

In the final chapter of the book we highlight each student's special successes and challenges. We also point out some of the "missed opportunities" along the way that could have aided each child and speculate on what the students might encounter in secondary school.

QUESTIONS FOR REFLECTION AND DISCUSSION

- In this chapter the authors highlighted that there is no simple path to acquiring "school" literacy. What is "school" literacy? What are examples of other literacies or background knowledge that students bring into the classroom? What are examples of other literacies or background knowledge that See Sing brought into the classroom?
- Review, reflect on, and discuss the possible questions a teacher may ponder during literacy instruction with emergent bilinguals. What additional questions do you have?
- In Table 1.2 the authors outline four central elements that interact for multilingual students as they learn to read and write in English. Define and discuss each element. What are or might be some challenges to each of these in practice? What are or might be some benefits of each in practice?
- What questions are you left with after reading Chapter 1? What are you excited to learn more about as you continue to read this book?

CHAPTER 2

From the Known to the New
Building Bridges Between Students and Their Schooling

It is the first week of school in an active 1st-grade classroom and Kevin glances around with wide eyes at the adults and children going about their work. Kevin is a Spanish-speaking, 6-year-old student who came to the United States with his mother shortly before the school year began. He speaks Spanish well and attended a kindergarten program in Mexico the previous year, so he knows what "being at school" means; he also has an initial understanding of print and how letters represent sounds in Spanish. At this moment, however, Kevin understands little of what is going on in class, what his teachers or peers say to him, or what he is expected to do. Kevin epitomizes being a **newcomer** to schooling in the United States.

In this chapter we focus on what students bring to school and what they encounter there that is different or unknown to them. Linguistically diverse students, including students who speak a language other than English at home, may bring a little or a lot of schooling in another language; transnational, **migrant** or refugee experiences; and cultural ways of being from their homes and communities that may vary significantly from the norms of the traditional classroom setting. Our essential dilemma examines how educators can build bridges between what students bring and the academic standards they are expected to achieve when students' background knowledge does not match school expectations.

> **Essential Dilemma:** What if students' background knowledge does not match the expectations teachers and administrators historically have held?

BEING A NEWCOMER

The idea of being a newcomer has influenced the way many schools operate as they attempt to accommodate students from varied educational, linguistic, and geographical backgrounds into mainstream classroom settings.

Some districts set up special classrooms or schools for students like Kevin who are new to the United States and are just beginning to learn English.

Newcomer programs aim to meet the academic and transitional needs of newly arrived immigrant children by providing specially designed instruction in which students learn academic content and language at the same time (Center for Research on Education, Diversity & Excellence, 2001). Specially designed programs for English learners use approaches described as sheltered instruction, integrated English language development, or specially designed academic instruction in English (Dutro, Núñez, & Helman, 2016; Peregoy & Boyle, 2012) with the goal of providing meaningful instruction in the content areas (social studies, math, science) and ELD in a synchronous way. This approach sometimes can be enacted as a program in a separate space from mainstream classrooms (often called "pull out"), but also can provide support for students within the general education classroom ("push in"). Specially designed instruction most typically is provided by ELL specialist teachers or bilingual educational assistants with the goal of accelerating student growth in language and content areas in order to transition students to mainstream settings and classrooms. Rather than providing a simplified, watered-down curriculum for English learners, specially designed instruction allows students access to rigorous grade-level materials through a variety of teaching methods that make the content more accessible. The teacher infuses activities that develop reading, writing, listening, and speaking in the English language.

In 1st grade, Kevin was assigned to a Language Academy classroom for students who were new to the country or who had minimal language proficiency in English (see Chapter 6 for a more detailed description of this type of classroom). His teachers had specialized training in setting goals for English language development for students at the beginning levels of proficiency and in creating curriculum that would be easier for students to understand. Nonetheless, Kevin's teacher described his early days in 1st grade as challenging because he seemed lost. Kevin tried to tell his teacher when another student took his blocks but, as she reported, "you could tell he just didn't have the words to tell me." One day Kevin got on the wrong bus after school, and when his family couldn't find him, they were very upset. Once the situation was resolved, his family printed out a large tag for him to keep with him that had his bus number on it. These two events highlight the disorientation that students like Kevin carry with them when they enter a school conducted in an unfamiliar language.

Tong was another student we observed throughout elementary school. He had already been in preschool and kindergarten in the United States before entering the 1st-grade Language Academy class. He came to 1st grade being able to read a solid group of sight words and knew most letters and sounds in English, but didn't seem to be able to use that knowledge to read books at his grade level. Tong's teacher described him as friendly and talkative; he was interested in playing games, especially with adults in the classroom. She described what she noticed about Tong's language: He would speak in sentences that kept going and going, but were poorly articulated and missing key vocabulary. Then Tong would look at the teacher as if to say, "Are you understanding?" She reflected, "I don't know if he is aware that he is hard to understand and I don't know if he is hard to understand in Hmong or not. That would be a good question I could ask a parent at conferences."

LINGUISTICALLY DIVERSE ELEMENTARY STUDENTS

Kevin and Tong represent two of the many profiles of linguistic diversity for students who speak languages or varieties of English at home other than standardized academic English. In the large city school district where Kevin and Tong attended school, approximately 75% of the population was students of color, and 41% were identified as English language learners. The most common languages other than English spoken in students' homes were Hmong, Spanish, and several African languages, but district families used 126 different home languages. Trends in the district over the past 25 years show a 240% increase in the number of English learners; the number of home languages spoken within the district increased in part because of refugee immigration relating to global catastrophic events.

The demographics for Kevin and Tong's district reflect national trends that show a 158% increase in the population 5 years and older who spoke a language other than English at home over a 20-year period ending in 2010 (Ryan, 2013). Your school district's demographics may follow this trend as well. Your students may come from one or two main groups of home languages or from 100 or more. Or, perhaps the linguistically diverse students you work with speak a nonstandardized variety of English, such as **African American English,** that varies in part from the sounds, grammar, and interaction norms or **pragmatics** of what students experience in the classroom setting. In this chapter you will be asked to think deeply about the background experiences that linguistically diverse students bring when they enter school and to investigate how you might use these experiences to support standards-based goals in literacy.

READY TO LEARN

In current educational reform initiatives, the concept of being "ready" for school and the academic tasks presented therein has become a key goal. Preschoolers need to be "ready" for kindergarten, kindergartners need to be "ready" for 1st grade, 3rd-graders need to be "ready" for rigorous content in the upper grades, and high schoolers need to be "ready" for college

(Strive Together Network, 2015). In many communities, parents are asked to bring their children to a "round-up" prior to the beginning of school to assess students on their readiness for the content of the upcoming year. In a number of states, students are "held back" in 3rd grade, before entering the upper elementary grades, if they have not met proficiency levels in reading (Rose & Schimke, 2012).

This "ready to learn" mindset implies that somehow students, and by association their parents, are deficient and need to be improved before they can be welcomed into their age-appropriate school setting. It suggests that the school curriculum is designed only for a one-size-fits-all clientele. The opposite of a readiness mindset for learning is one that sees students as rich cultural beings who come to school ready to learn no matter their previous experiences. This mindset was stated eloquently by P. David Pearson (2007):

> Kids are who they are.
> They know what they know.
> They bring what they bring.
> Wishing they knew something more or something different won't make it so. Our job as teachers is to help them transform what they bring into curricular resources rather than instructional inconveniences. (p. 56)

It is clear that students bring diverse linguistic, cultural, socioeconomic, and academic resources with them to school. Educators and institutional policies must begin to acknowledge and plan for the differences in background experiences and education that students bring to their academic setting, and to use the strengths that students have to provide rigorous learning environments under "their watch" each year (Genishi & Dyson, 2009). As the professionals, it is incumbent on educators to plot a successful course for all students who enter their doors, regardless of whether they are deemed "ready."

Kevin did not know English when he entered school in the United States, but he was ready to learn language and literacy skills in a new language in his 1st-grade learning community. Tong had the foundations of early alphabetic skills and brought excitement about his academic journey as well as pride in his family and Hmong heritage. In their cases, as well as so many others around the country, it was not the students who needed to be ready, but rather the teachers and schools that received them.

WHAT STUDENTS BRING TO SCHOOL

Students are not blank slates when they enter school for the first time or each time they enroll. For the most part, all students bring the ability to communicate with family members and friends; they know how to interact with members of their linguistic and cultural communities; they bring the combined wisdom of their experiences and what has been passed down to them from their elders; and, most important, they bring with them the love of their families who aspire for them to succeed at school.

Language Resources

Kevin may have known only a handful of words in English when he started 1st grade, but he had plenty of language resources that he used regularly and effectively with people who spoke Spanish. Kevin could communicate his wants and needs, understand stories, sing songs, tell jokes, and even begin to sound out simple words in print. At home he could keep up with the flow of conversation, comprehend what was expected of him, and contribute his own ideas in a culturally appropriate manner. Family members could see Kevin's strengths because he could express himself with language they understood. In the English-only environment of school, however, he was not able to show his competencies as clearly. Table 2.1 highlights some of the discrepancies in how Kevin's language resources were viewed at home and at school.

As Kevin moved from home to school, he must have felt a strong shift from a setting in which he was known and understood through language, to a setting that was hard to figure out and where most people did not understand his capabilities. The concept of being known (Chhuon & Wallace, 2012) and how teachers work toward this goal with their students is discussed more fully in Chapter 4.

Table 2.1. Perceptions of Kevin's Language Skills at Home and at School

At Home	At School
Was able to communicate wants and needs.	"Did not have the words."
Received comprehensible information.	Was dependent on peers who spoke Spanish to interpret what was going on.
Was expected to respond to and interact with what others requested.	Was perceived as not being able to understand ideas because he did not have the English words.
Was a full member of the community.	Was an "English learner" who could not fully engage with the classroom community.
Was a "whole" and capable person.	Was not yet "ready" for what school offered.

Background Experiences and Academic Capabilities

Kevin and Tong came to 1st grade in the Language Academy classroom with distinct sets of previous experiences. Table 2.2 highlights elements of their background and academic experiences.

As Table 2.2 outlines, Tong was born in the United States and attended preschool and kindergarten in English. He spoke Hmong fluently with family, friends, and community members. Kevin used Spanish fluently; he had come to the United States recently and had fewer English language resources. He brought early literacy knowledge in Spanish that he could transfer to other alphabetic writing systems. Both students knew "how to do" school in the sense that they previously had been a part of classroom settings with teachers who guided them through learning activities and structured peer interactions.

Cultural Ways of Being and Interacting

Every person has been apprenticed into the world through their interactions with significant people in their lives. Humans are social and **cultural**, and diversity is a hallmark of our species. Tong and Kevin came from families and cultures that held certain values and styles of interaction. Their parents guided them to behave in certain ways with adults, siblings or peers, and teachers. Outside of school, both students were an integral part of a large network of extended family and community that worked together to accomplish tasks necessary for group survival and success.

Table 2.2. Kevin's and Tong's Experiences Prior to 1st Grade

	Kevin	Tong
Home language competency	Fluent and capable speaker of Spanish.	Fluent and capable speaker of Hmong.
English language competency	Immigrated to United States with mother shortly before 1st grade started. Knew very few English words. Level 1 on standardized assessment (most limited designation).	Born in United States to a family that had been refugees. Level 1 on standardized assessment (most limited designation), but scored near the top of that category.
Previous schooling	Attended a preschool and kindergarten program in Mexico in Spanish.	Attended preschool and kindergarten in the United States in English.
Early literacy knowledge	Had beginning knowledge of the Spanish letter and sound system.	Knew the majority of letter names and sounds in English. Identified beginning sounds and rhymes.

It must have been quite disconcerting for these students to enter a traditional classroom setting where work is created and evaluated person by person and individual accomplishment is prioritized. We discuss these ideas through the lens of **culturally relevant pedagogy** in Chapter 4 and describe how it applies to linguistically diverse students such as the students highlighted here.

BUILDING ON WHAT STUDENTS KNOW

Throughout this book you will be asked to consider ways to build on the knowledge, experiences, and attitudes that students bring to the classroom. Instead of seeing students as *lacking* what they need for success or *not being ready* for classroom content, an asset-based mindset positions students as capable and complex. It validates their life experiences, languages, and the aspirations of their families and communities.

Step 1: Find Out What Students Bring

A first step to building a bridge to new learning is to know where to anchor the connection. Figure 2.1 highlights the idea that understanding students' resources, or **funds of knowledge**, gives teachers avenues to engage with standards-based curriculum goals (Moll & González, 1994).

On the left side of the bridge is a list of some of the assets that all students bring to school. On the right side are the goals toward which educators work. Because this book focuses on literacy and language learning, we have

Figure 2.1. Linking Student Background Knowledge to Curriculum

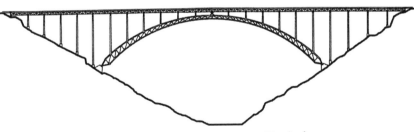

Students' Resources
- Languages
- Cultural values
- Knowledge of the world
- School experiences
- Interests and goals

Curriculum
- Grade-level language arts standards
- Disciplinary inquiry units
- Becoming bilingual

noted learning the grade-level language arts standards as a primary goal. In addition, literacy is integrated throughout disciplinary content, in which students face more and more complex academic vocabulary (see Chapter 3). We add "becoming bilingual" as a curricular target as well. Students who bring a home language or variation of standardized academic English to the classroom deserve to keep the language they bring even as they become more fully proficient in standardized English. In this way they can continue to maintain full participation in the **discourse communities** of their home cultures. Neglecting or attempting to erase a home language takes away academic and social power from students. Being bilingual creates **metalinguistic awareness** about languages, helps people learn additional languages more easily, increases executive functioning skills, opens the door to new people and ideas, and makes a person more marketable in the job pool (Rodríguez, Carrasquillo, & Lee, 2014).

Some key questions to help you find out what your students bring to school include: What languages or variations of English do your students speak outside of school? What background knowledge do your students bring? In what ways do your students use literacy with their families and friends? What values do your students and their families hold most dear? What do your students know that you *don't* know? These and similar questions can be a starting place for reflecting on your students' resources.

If you have shared out-of-school experiences with your students and their families, you may already be able to answer some of the questions listed above. If you haven't, consider some of the following "getting to know you" activities in class or during school–family events:

- Create "All About Me" books where students share their interests, family life, and background experiences.
- Send home cameras for students to take pictures of the people, places, and things in their lives that they are most proud of.
- Create writing assignments in which students share their out-of-school lives, values, and friends and family.
- Encourage students to share their writing, songs, and stories in their home language.
- Survey students about their interests in and out of school.
- Bring in community liaisons who are members of your students' home language communities to facilitate cross-cultural discussions and sharing.

Throughout all of the activities noted above, it is important that you remain open and positive as students express their background experiences. Acknowledging students' funds of knowledge in a positive way will ensure that they continue to share who they are and what they know with you.

Step 2: Identify What May Be Unknown to Students

Earlier in this chapter we noted what students bring to school and the potential "disconnect" with what they encounter there. In Chapter 4 we present an extended discussion of how culturally relevant teaching with students from linguistically diverse backgrounds provides a solid avenue to strengthen student–teacher relationships and, in turn, has a powerful impact on student success at school. In this section we want to share a different example of a potential obstacle to student success that we found as we followed the students—learning the sounds and syntax of English.

Language differences. Languages vary in a number of ways in their sound and spelling patterns, and oral and written language samples can be a window into what students know of a language and its writing system (Bear, Invernizzi, Templeton, & Johnston, 2016; Henderson, 1981). For this reason, "errors" should not be seen as mistakes, but rather as a sign of development. Through the 6 years of observations of our focal students, we collected oral and written language samples to help us understand their accomplishments and their challenges in literacy development in English. Table 2.3 presents some examples of their oral and written language through the grade levels. In our examples we use capital letters to represent students' developmental spellings and quotations to share what they verbalize.

In the first column of Table 2.3 we highlight some of the ways that the languages of Tong (Hmong speaker) and Kevin (Spanish speaker) differ from English. Tong's language of Hmong is a **tonal language**, spoken by a community of people who live in southern China, Burma, northern Thailand, Laos, and Vietnam, and who, beginning in the 1970s, emigrated to other parts of the world, including the United States. Hmong words end with a vowel sound and each has a tone. The tone of a Hmong word is noted by one of seven consonant markers (b, m, j, v, s, g, d) or no letter (McGinn & McMenamin, 1984). Nasal sounds such as /n/ or /ng/ are frequent in Hmong, and as we worked with students from that language background we sometimes noticed that they would include extra *n*s and *ng*s in their writing. As an example of this, you will note in the second column of Table 2.3 that Tong spelled the word *dream*, one of the words on the Qualitative Spelling Inventory (Bear et al., 2016), as GING throughout his 1st-, 2nd-, and 3rd-grade years. It appears that Tong's perception of sounds in English words has been filtered by the sounds he knew best from the Hmong language.

Another potential linguistic challenge across languages is **syntax**, how words are put together into phrases and sentences, and **morphology**, the way that words are constructed using meaningful chunks. In the Hmong language, words are not **inflected** as they are in English. Instead of adding an -s to make *car* into *cars*, in the Hmong language a new word would be added: *car + many*

Table 2.3. Oral and Written Language Samples

How the Home Language Contrasts with English	Language Samples
Student: Tong **Home Language: Hmong**	
• Tones communicate meaning and also are noted in the written word. • Some English sounds are not present (e.g., /th/, /r/, most consonant blends). • Nasal sounds such as /n/ and /m/ precede most consonant clusters. • Being a tonal language, the final letter (b, m, j, v, s, g, d) signifies the correct tone to use. Words are composed of open syllables that end with vowel sounds (with appropriate tones). • Uses more than one word to express inflection (e.g., *car + many*; *walk + yesterday*). • Noun–adjective order is reversed (*cat black* instead of *black cat*).	• Developmentally spells: » *dream* as GING (1st to 3rd grades) » *rainbow* as RING BOY (2nd grade) » *drive* as TRITH (4th grade) » *different* as DIFFLE (5th grade) » *scary* as SARY (6th grade) » *stole* as STORLE (6th grade) • Says: » "reet" for *street* (2nd grade) » "have" for *has* (4th grade) • Writes: » I LIKE SIE NI OSIT SIN IS COEN. [I like sitting outside is cold.] (2nd grade) » I DONE for *I'm done* (3rd grade) • 1st-grade syntax sample: » "I stand up and be quiet and I not screaming and I not running."
Student: Kevin **Home Language: Spanish**	
• Vowel sounds are distinct from English (e.g., Spanish *e* has a similar sound to English *a*). • Some English sounds are not present (e.g., /sh/, /v/). • S-blends do not begin words (e.g., *estampa* not *stamp*). • A limited set of consonants may end words (e.g., /b/, /g/, /t/); consonant blends not permitted. • Noun–adjective order is generally reversed (*cat black* instead of *black cat*).	• Developmentally spells: » *gum* as KOM (1st grade) » *friend* as FRAN (2nd grade) » *checkers* as SHAKRS (2nd grade) » *fright* as FRITE (3rd grade) » *shopping* as SHOPING (4th grade) • Says: » "she's mom" for *her mom* (1st grade) » "observate" for *observe* (3rd grade) • Writes: » THE MOUS IS IN THE SKUO [The mouse is in the school.] (1st grade) » I WANT TO LET THE BEES OUT BECAUSE THERE WILL BE MORE FLOWERS BECAUSE BEES GIVE POLEN ON THE FLOWER (4th grade) • 1st-grade syntax sample: » "Cards, Go Fish, and, and, and . . . coloring . . . and books and . . . done."

= more than one car. Instead of adding -ed to a word to show it was done in the past as in *walked*, in Hmong another word would be added following the verb, such as *walk + yesterday*. As we interviewed teachers and worked with students over the years, we heard about and saw examples of Hmong students who had difficulty saying the inflectional endings of English words, such as the -s in *cars* or the -ed in *walked* (McGinn & McMenamin, 1984). One district we worked with had an extended controversy about whether these miscues should count against students on their reading passage assessments or their oral language tests. Clearly, this presented a linguistic challenge that influenced literacy practices for Hmong students.

The Spanish language, as noted in the first column of Table 2.3, also varies in sounds and syntax from English. Vowels have different sounds than their English counterparts in ways that can be confusing to a novice reader and writer from a Spanish language background. For example, the *e* in Spanish has the sound of the letter name *a* in English, and the letter *i* in Spanish has the sound of the letter name *e* in English (Helman, 2004). In qualitative reviews of Spanish speakers' developmental spelling in English, the substitution of these vowels appears—even for students who have never received formal instruction in written Spanish (Helman, 2005). There are a number of consonant sounds that also can be tricky for Spanish speakers learning to read and write in English (Helman, 2004). One example is the use of /sh/ and /ch/. In the Spanish language, *sh* is not a digraph with a distinct sound as in the word *shell*. Spanish speakers may have a hard time differentiating the sound of /sh/ from /ch/, as Kevin did when he wrote SHAKRS for *checkers*, as noted in Table 2.3.

The Spanish language also varies from English in grammatical ways. For example, noun–adjective order generally is reversed as in *gato negro* instead of *black cat*. Spanish-speaking students may say, "See the house red," as they are learning to transpose their grammatical way of thinking onto English. Across languages, sentences may use distinct forms and verbs to communicate the same ideas, so, for example, a Spanish-speaking student may say, "I have 7 years," instead of, "I am 7 years old." Students learning English as a new language may make miscues with prepositions as well, as Kevin did when he said, ". . . because bees give pollen on the flowers."

Learning about students' home languages. Elementary teachers bring a range of linguistic experiences to their jobs in the classroom. Some teachers speak one or more languages besides English, and others are monolingual English speakers. Some teachers learned standardized academic English for the first time when they entered school, while others moved seamlessly between the language spoken in their home and that of mainstream classroom instruction. Given this great variety of background experiences, it is no wonder that a lot of teachers question how they can learn about the variety of home languages that students bring to the classroom. Teachers often ask, "What if I do not speak the same languages as my students?" Some teachers lament, "I have students from so many language backgrounds in my classroom, how can I learn about all of them so I understand their difficulties?" Following are a few tips that we have shared in our work with teachers to help them get to know their students' home languages without feeling overwhelmed by the task.

- Identify early on in the school year what languages your students speak through conversations or "get to know you" surveys with students or their families.
- Select one of the predominant languages that your students speak as a place to begin your learning. Explore online some of the language resource websites to find out more about the language and the people who speak it. Many of these resource books or websites also highlight how the language differs from English in sounds, morphology, or syntax.
- If you know a lot about the language that predominates in your classroom, move to the next most common language. If you focus on one language each year, you can increase your knowledge of the world's languages and be better prepared to understand the challenges of your diverse students in the future.
- Make a simple chart for yourself highlighting what is similar and what is different between the language you are researching and English. What is common between students' home language and English? What sounds and grammatical processes do you think will be most difficult for your students? Knowing these details will help you to work with the commonalities first.
- Consider talking with community liaisons from the school or bilingual family members to check out your perceptions of the contrasts in languages. Students in the upper elementary grades also can be a wonderful resource to help you explore characteristics of their home languages.

Most of the recommendations presented above take very little extra planning time from a teacher's busy schedule. If your region finds that it is enrolling increasing numbers of new students from a particular linguistic group, district personnel sometimes create materials to share with teaching staff to help them learn about their students' linguistic and cultural backgrounds. Finding out this information also may be a good topic for study within a **professional learning community (PLC)** or as a goal for an individual teacher's yearly professional development plan.

Step 3: Connect Students' Funds of Knowledge to the Curricula

In Step 1 you identified what your students bring to school in the way of language and literacy knowledge. In Step 2 you learned about what is similar across languages, and what is different. Step 3 of this process involves connecting to what students already know and what can be easily transferred to their understanding of oral and/or written English. Below are several examples of ways to do this:

- What sounds exist in both the home language and English? Use those to begin your alphabet study.
- How are letters formed? Begin with the ones that are common to both languages.
- Are there words that have similar sounds or spellings and meanings (cognates)? Point these out and use them early on in reading and writing activities. Create cognate charts related to the themes you study in class.
- What kinds of stories are told or written in students' home languages? Ask students to share them in various ways. Encourage students to **code mesh** by inserting words or phrases from their home languages into their stories when those words paint better pictures. Then, take the time to ask what these words mean; they will be windows for you into students' background experiences.

It may seem impossible to find linguistic commonalities when students' oral and written languages are very different from English. For example, a student's language may use a logographic writing system that moves from right to left and has no apparent cognates with English. Where will the commonalities be? There is no question that this will be a challenge; to begin, take a step back and think about what you have learned about the student's home language. The writing systems of both English and the student's home language represent oral language written down—an important conceptual understanding. Although the directionality may be different, it will be consistently structured. As students speak, listen to the sounds and rhythms of their language. Identify the sounds that should be easy for them to pronounce, and study English words that begin with those sounds first. Assess whether students have any literacy skills in the home language, and watch them write or draw to see what you learn about their strengths. Look for children's books in their home languages to share in class. See what the students can tell you about their language by looking over these print materials together.

Step 4: Move to the New and Challenging

In the final step to building bridges between what students bring to school and the academic expectations they are expected to accomplish, teachers need to go beyond what is common and accessible to students, and address the curriculum that is distinct and challenging. This is the time for you to use all of the **pedagogical content knowledge** that you have gathered in courses and prior teaching experiences to make sure that you are using efficient, effective, and evidence-based teaching practices so that your students can readily understand the material. Emergent bilingual students have a lot to learn to meet the standards, and there is no time to waste using less than the best teaching practices. In the next section, we return to the example of learning the sounds and syntax of English, and how to approach what is hard or confusing to students as they read, write, and speak in a new language.

Addressing cross-linguistic challenges. To this point in our discussion, we have suggested that teachers learn about their students, identify what may be unknown to them in the English language or disciplinary content, begin teaching based on commonalities between the new and the known, and, last, move to the unknown or distinct. Table 2.3 highlighted several cross-linguistic challenges for students who speak Spanish at home and are learning to read and write in English at school, such as the differences in the sounds and names of vowels, or new sounds in the language being learned. One specific example that can help make this conversation more concrete is the case of the /sh/ sound for Spanish-speaking students.

Figure 2.2 is a drawing and story that Kevin made in October of his 2nd-grade year. At this point, Kevin had been in school in the United States for a full year, and his early writing skills were coming along very well. From this writing sample you can see that Kevin developed excellent alphabetic skills in that year: He represents most of the sounds in the sentence he has written, and his text is very readable to the average 1st- or 2nd-grade teacher ["I was playing with my friend checkers."]. Kevin was able to use what he knew about Spanish letters and sounds and apply those to his writing in English. For example, if you use the Spanish letter sounds to read the way he spells *my* [MAY], it makes perfect sense.

Notice how Kevin spells *checkers* as SHAKRS. All of the sounds are represented, and this is great for an alphabetic-level, "spelling by sound" student. Kevin perceives the /sh/ and /ch/ sound to be one and the same, so in his work, and that of other Spanish-speaking students, these two sounds often are interchanged (Helman, 2004). The sh/ch contrast is a prime example of a cross-linguistic challenge that could be either addressed explicitly in class or left for students to figure out on their own. Students who are not given explicit support to identify cross-linguistic differences and time to practice using the features correctly may never understand what they are doing incorrectly or how to master the new language. It is incumbent on teachers to guide them in this process.

Teaching practices that support cross-linguistic learning. Helman (2009) has outlined four areas of strategic teaching to support emergent bilinguals' learning: (1) engaging in a learning community, (2) explicit and systematic

Figure 2.2. Kevin's Writing Sample

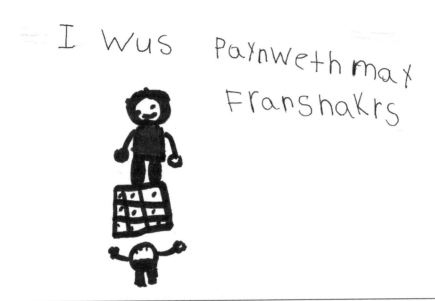

I wus Paynweth max Franshakrs

instruction, (3) highlighting connections, and (4) actively constructing new knowledge. We offer one example of each kind of strategy below to get you thinking about how Kevin's understanding of the /sh/ and /ch/ sounds in English could be supported to help fine-tune his alphabetic writing skills.

- *Engaging in a learning community:* One aspect of a safe learning community is that it should be a low-anxiety environment where students feel comfortable expressing themselves without being subjected to ridicule. To identify fine distinctions in sound, such as the sh/ch contrast, students need time to articulate and get feedback on their pronunciations in supportive ways. Being able to say and differentiate these sounds will enable students to improve their writing skills. An effective teacher will find fun and informal ways to help Kevin, and students with similar needs, to practice their pronunciations without being put on the spot in front of peers. One idea to consider: Use several /sh/ and /ch/ words such as *chew, chop, chin, check, shoe, shell, shop,* or *ship* to create an engaging chant for students to sing as a group.
- *Explicit and systematic instruction:* The curriculum that students experience in class needs to be clear and understandable. Students need opportunities to see what they are learning modeled, engage in their own practice, and get feedback. Explicit instruction on the

sh/ch contrast might involve doing a word and picture sort using items that begin with *sh* or *ch*. The teacher shows a picture of an item, for example, *shoe*, asks students to repeat the word, matches the printed word to its picture, and then helps students to sort it into the correct sh or ch group. After participating in a modeled sort, students have an opportunity to classify on their own or with a partner and get feedback from the teacher (Helman, Bear, Invernizzi, Templeton, & Johnston, 2009).

- *Highlighting connections:* Teachers help students highlight connections when they provide opportunities for students to reflect on how new learning relates to what they already know. This can happen by talking about how English is different from the home language, sharing personal experiences or background knowledge, or using graphic organizers. Spanish-speaking students can be encouraged to think aloud about how the /sh/ sound is different than sounds in Spanish. In small groups of fellow Spanish speakers, they can share strategies they use to identify and correctly represent the /sh/ sound in their reading and writing.

- *Actively constructing new knowledge:* Learning becomes internalized when students put it into practice in purposeful and varied ways. Students who have lots of opportunities to write using their own developmental spelling will authentically practice writing words with *sh* and *ch*, and teachers can conference with students who substitute one for the other. To structure a lesson that ensures students will encounter words with *sh* and *ch*, teachers could formulate a writing prompt such as: "What should children always do?" In order to respond to the prompt, students will need to use *sh* and *ch* several times.

We share the above depictions of teaching not because they are all-inclusive; nor do we want to imply that all students will need to experience so many kinds of instruction around a particular skill. Rather, we present these examples to demonstrate how to help students learn something that does not fit into their current schemata and thus may cause confusion. Clear instruction in a safe learning environment, with opportunities to reflect on

Teaching Opportunity: Look over the four areas for strategically supporting linguistically diverse students in their learning. Each day in your teaching think of one thing you could do that would help students to better understand information that is dissimilar from what they already know.

previous knowledge and practice the new skill with support, will provide students with a much better chance of gaining knowledge that is currently unfamiliar.

DILEMMAS AND OPPORTUNITIES

In the next section we reflect upon particular aspects of Kevin's and Tong's academic journeys, discussing the linguistic support or lack of support these two creative and complex boys—whom you will continue to read about in other chapters—received as they participated in mainstream classrooms in English. This reflection is not a comprehensive telling of Tong's and Kevin's stories, but rather highlights relevant points regarding the chapter's focus of guiding students from the known to the new.

Reflecting on Tong's Academic Journey

Tong began 1st grade with a firm home language (Hmong) and a beginning level of English. He was an outgoing and social boy who bonded easily with adults. Probably because of his emergent skills in English, in the early grades Tong frequently used observation as a way to "know what to do in class." For example, in a whole-group lesson that we observed in his 2nd-grade classroom, the teacher described step-by-step what she wanted students to write or draw on their papers. Tong would watch the person next to him, do the same thing, and follow the directions that way. He had found a way to accomplish the task when his linguistic skills were not adequate. We also observed that during class Tong interacted primarily with peers who spoke Hmong.

Tong began 1st grade with good phonological and early alphabetic skills in English, and our team expected that this head start would help him learn to read and write in a fairly straightforward way. As we watched his progress between 1st and 3rd grades, however, we realized that his language and literacy development would not be simple. By 2nd grade Tong's progress began to plateau. In the spring he was not able to decode rapidly and was challenged by blending and segmenting sounds in words he decoded or wrote. He read at a pre-primer (early 1st-grade) level, and his developmental spelling inventory showed that he was using his alphabetic skills to represent some of the sounds in words. For example, he spelled *pet* as PAT and *blade* as BAD. He scored a level 3 out of 5 on a measure of oral English—an early intermediate designation. In 3rd grade and beyond, the gap between Tong's achievement levels and the grade-level expectations continued to widen. By the end of 5th grade, despite several years of interventions and ELL service, he was reading at an end-of-2nd-grade level, although he was classified as a "proficient English speaker" on the district's measure of oral English. His spelling inventory showed that he was able to move beyond simple spelling–sound correspondences but was making errors with final -e markers, vowel digraphs, and inflected endings. Tong epitomizes the dilemma frequently seen with emergent bilingual students—it was fairly easy for him to develop the early code-based reading skills, but more difficult for him to tackle the more advanced aspects of literacy practice (Lesaux

& Geva, 2006). Despite his limited academic achievement, Tong retained his enthusiasm and interest in school.

Our team reviewed the data we had collected on Tong and at times had serious conversations with his teachers about what was holding him back from fluent and proficient reading and writing. Our analysis showed that he never quite acquired accuracy in using the English phonics system. Was the difficulty for him related to a cross-linguistic confusion between the tonal language of Hmong and the new language of English? We do not know. His teachers did discuss in a general way some of the typical difficulties they saw with their Hmong speakers, but did not connect these challenges to Tong in particular.

Relating our dilemma with Tong to this chapter's focus on helping to bridge students' linguistic, cultural, and academic knowledge to the new content they experience in the classroom, we wondered what opportunities for support might be identified for him in particular. Figure 2.3 suggests a few ideas that might have helped him better understand the phonological and writing system of English. It is organized into the four categories of support strategies that we shared above.

Tong represents one profile of an emergent bilingual student. His teachers worked hard and did their best, but something was missing to help him succeed. His journey brought up many questions that have yet to be answered about the role of cross-linguistic challenges and what kind of instruction might have helped him bridge these linguistic differences.

Figure 2.3. Potential Cross-Linguistic Supports for Tong

Engaging in a learning community

- Have students discuss differences across languages with classmates and teachers.
- Develop routines that require both partners to do the work during an activity.
- Conduct brief informal language assessments.

Highlighting connections

- Print labels on pictures that contain "tricky" sounds to make an oral–print connection.
- Provide opportunities for students to reflect orally or in writing on what they know and don't know.
- Share common errors and discuss them as a group.

Explicit and systematic instruction

- Sort words and pictures that use the sounds of English most difficult for Hmong-speaking students.
- Post charts to clarify English letters and sounds.
- Use notebooks, reference materials, or study aids to reinforce the English writing system.

Actively constructing new knowledge

- Provide clues to understanding unfamiliar skills using rhythm and body movements.
- Break away from the teacher asks–students answer routine, and let students do the asking.
- Help students use their new learning in authentic tasks.

Reflecting on Kevin's Academic Journey

Kevin began 1st grade with strong skills in the Spanish language and had attended preschool in Mexico. He knew only a handful of words in English when he began school in the United States. As a newcomer, Kevin had difficulty understanding much of what went on in class for the first few months. Still, his early literacy experiences in Spanish provided a bridge to the alphabetic instruction going on in the classroom.

In contrast to Tong, Kevin's literacy growth progressed steadily and hand-in-hand with his language learning. While he demonstrated common cross-linguistic confusions, such as the sh/ch uncertainty noted previously, these mix-ups faded away as he gained accuracy and fluency in reading. By 4th grade Kevin demonstrated knowledge of written patterns in English with words such as *bright* and *spoil*, and no cross-linguistic confusions were noted in his writing. Most likely, Kevin's interest and fluency in reading had helped him to firm up his understanding of the representation of sounds in English.

You will read more about a key dilemma in Kevin's learning trajectory in Chapter 4, when he lost connection with his 6th-grade teacher and almost failed that school year. In this chapter, we consider a missed opportunity from his early years of elementary school. This missed opportunity revolves around using Kevin's home language as a resource to build on.

Kevin came to the United States with strong Spanish language skills and a beginning understanding of phonics in Spanish. Over time and with the help of his mother, Kevin started to make connections between what he knew in Spanish and what he was learning in English. As he made these connections, his learning in English skyrocketed. We believe that if his teachers had intentionally connected his knowledge in Spanish with classroom objectives in English, this progress would have been even more substantial. Instead, as discussed more fully in Chapter 5, Kevin's mother was discouraged from working with him in Spanish at home. Although supporting students' conceptual and linguistic resources in a home language is a powerful way to empower students and accelerate their learning, many educators still mistakenly think that it will be detrimental to students' learning of academic English. Ending this subtractive practice is critical; educators should encourage parents to develop their children's home language resources to the fullest extent possible.

A missed cross-linguistic opportunity for Kevin would have involved helping him to see meaningful connections between words in English and Spanish. Cognates are useful bridges between knowledge that students already have and what they are learning. For example, when Kevin was studying about the community, it might have been helpful for him to compare words in English and Spanish, such as hospital/hospital, restaurant/restaurante, or supermarket/supermercado. If his teachers had built on what

Kevin knew in his home language, his curiosity about languages might have been sparked and his heritage validated. In addition, his academic skills and higher-order thinking could have been fortified.

SUMMARIZING LEARNING

In this chapter, we explored what it means to expect students to be "ready" for their age-appropriate classroom placement, and problematized that conceptual framework. We presented an asset-based perspective that moved from identifying the background experiences that students bring to school to building bridges to curricular goals. Educators can structure improved learning experiences for linguistically diverse students by: (1) finding out what students bring, (2) identifying what may be unknown for students, (3) developing curriculum that starts with what students know, and only then (4) moving to new and challenging academic expectations.

Kevin's and Tong's experiences demonstrated the potential for, as well as the challenges of, building bridges between what students bring to school and what they are expected to learn. Building on the experiences of these two students, as well as students in your own classrooms, you can learn to be conscientious and knowledgeable in creating pathways for your students from what they know to the academic goals at school.

QUESTIONS FOR REFLECTION AND DISCUSSION

- Figure 2.3 suggests some potential ways to support cross-linguistic learning for multilingual students. What ideas can you think of to add to this chart?
- Think of a time when you were unable to easily understand the language being spoken. What tools did you use to make cross-linguistic connections?
- Why is it important to help students become bilingual? What happens when schooling attempts to "erase" a student's home language?

CHAPTER 3

Learning Academic Language

Imagine a busy 1st-grade classroom early in the school year. In this classroom, there are 24 children from a variety of cultural and linguistic backgrounds, such as Somali, Latino, and Hmong, as well as native English speakers. Students go about literacy tasks while the teacher works with a small group of students at the back table. Along one wall, two girls, one Somali and the other Hmong, are "reading the room" with a heart-shaped pointer. Elsewhere, Spanish can be heard as two students page through a class-made book about their fieldtrip to a farm. To the side of the room, a lone Somali boy, Abdirahman, grabs a pack of word cards and proceeds to the center of the carpet area. He says to no one in particular and to anyone who will listen, "Who play with me?" In another corner, a Hmong boy, Chue, engages in reading a book at the listening center with a Hmong girl by his side. As he listens, he speaks loudly to the girl next to him. He places the headphones on her head and they converse in Hmong about the story they are enjoying in English.

The teacher in this classroom is knowledgeable about the role of language in literacy development and understands the need for her emergent bilingual students to have interactions with one another around written and oral text; she allows the children to use their first language to help them understand what they're hearing and reading. Her students benefit from time: time to practice and play, to listen and learn. And the teacher knows that for students who are learning English, this is especially true. It may be years before these children are using English in a manner similar to their peers, and they need time to develop it. She wants her classroom to be a place in which students are not pushed, but rather encouraged, to develop language proficiency as they encounter English directly through lessons and indirectly from the environment around them.

And yet, the teacher also knows that her students don't have much time. Her emergent bilingual students, some who have come to the United States just recently from refugee camps and limited schooling opportunities, are already years behind. There is no time to wait on language, especially academic language. It is urgent that children make tremendous gains in their language and literacy during the elementary years, at least 1½ years every

> **Essential Dilemma:** Language learning takes time, but waiting for it to develop positions students farther and farther behind.

school year in order to keep up with their native English-speaking peers (Collier & Thomas, 2004). This 1st-grade teacher is faced with a powerful contradiction and another of the essential dilemmas of developing English language and literacy: Deep learning of academic language takes time, but there is no time to wait. Emergent bilingual students must begin as quickly as possible to learn the language they need to be academically successful.

In this chapter we examine the growth of academic language and its link to literacy learning through the examples of two students, Abdirahman and Chue. The journeys of these two boys will help us consider several of the issues that surface relating to academic language, and the ways their teachers found to make their time in school as productive as possible.

ABOUT ACADEMIC LANGUAGE

Anyone who has learned a new language has experienced the difference between *social* language and *academic* language. A face-to-face conversation with a store clerk about the price of a chocolate bar is likely to be much more comprehensible than, say, a discussion on how the habitat of the bald eagles in North America has been impacted by climate change over the past 5 years. Why? Because the language used in the chocolate conversation is *highly contextualized* and *cognitively undemanding*. In other words, it is usually easier to communicate in another language if you're talking about something that is "right there" in the environment, that you can see or experience, and about a concept that can be grasped directly. Most social conversations fall into this category and also tend to occur face-to-face so that if there is confusion, the speaker can modify his or her speech to ensure that the listener understands.

The language used in academic contexts is often highly decontextualized and cognitively demanding, and has a formal tone—quite the opposite of social language. When students are learning about rainforest ecosystems in a classroom, for example, they are likely to encounter technical vocabulary and unfamiliar phrases and sentences such as in this short paragraph:

> The tallest trees scattered throughout the rain forest are called emergents. There are usually only one or two of these towering trees (115 to 250 feet tall) per acre. . . . Birds, such as the toucan and the macaw, find refuge and a bird's-eye view of the forest in these treetops. (Audet, Gibson, & Flag, 1995, p. 27)

Note some of the unusual language use in this sample text, such as "emergents" as a noun to give more information about the towering trees. In addition, the text incorporates rare words such as "toucan" and "find refuge." The last sentence in the paragraph contains another phrase that tells more about the subject (birds)—"such as the toucan and the macaw"—that complicates the sentence structure. It is easy to see how in a few short sentences a student learning English could find herself lost and confused even if she is able to read the text.

Academic language can be defined most concisely as "the specialized language, both oral and written, of academic settings that facilitates communication and thinking about disciplinary content" (Nagy & Townsend, 2012, p. 92). **Academic language proficiency** is more than just knowing the language; it's also knowing when and how to use language the right way. It's like being able to look in your tackle box for the right lure to reel in the big catch, rather than just throwing in a hook and line.

It often requires 6 or more years to gain proficiency in academic English (Hakuta, Butler, & Witt, 2000). Why does it take so long to acquire this form of language? Exposure to social English at school and even in students' communities and via the media occurs at a much higher rate than exposure to academic English. Many teachers initially focus on supporting conversational English, such as helping students learn to get lunch in the cafeteria, converse with their peers during classroom tasks, and answer basic questions. Children learn social language quickly because they use it to make friends and get their immediate needs met. Academic English is not used as frequently outside of school settings. Emergent bilinguals may get few opportunities to engage with others about the big ideas and abstract concepts that require the use of academic language. There is also a danger that once students gain a level of social proficiency, their teachers may not see a need for continued language instruction. To understand more about academic language learning, we explore the school literacy and language development of Abdirahman and Chue.

TWO STUDENTS LEARNING ENGLISH

Abdirahman and Chue both started 1st grade with very little knowledge of spoken or written English. Like the other children featured in this book, they both scored in the "non-English speaker" range on a standardized oral language assessment at the beginning of their 1st-grade year. Yet, as highlighted in the scenario at the beginning of the chapter, they used and explored language in varied ways. In this chapter, we use these two boys' stories as windows for better understanding academic language learning. We also investigate ways that teachers can incorporate the instruction of academic language into their curriculum.

Abdirahman

In the primary grades, it appeared that Abdirahman's strong verbal skills supported his emerging English literacy skills. Abdirahman's verbal processing of the ideas going through his head and his attempts to use English in social settings (as seen in the chapter-opening vignette) made it easier for his teachers to assess his abilities. Still, in a manner similar to other emergent bilinguals, as he moved forward in the elementary grades, his academic language did not keep pace with his social language or his desire to express the content he was learning.

Abdirahman's limited prior schooling experiences led teachers to focus initially on his behavior in class. Classroom observations conducted in his first 2 years in the United States show him to be very eager to know what was happening in his environment as he acquired knowledge of what school was about. In a large group, he often was mesmerized as he watched what was being presented, and responded to lessons using his whole body. He frequently was unaware of others' personal space, but when asked to "rein in" his actions, he responded promptly. His motor skills, demonstrated by cutting and coloring, were still developing. He would struggle to write his name correctly and in the space provided. His English oral communication consisted of short phrases and very simple questions. Yet his 1st-grade teacher at the time explained, "He just reads and reads and reads and he is so proud of that stack of books he loves to read. We wrote about our trip to the farm and he wrote his own sentence: "I know that I now know that cows eat hay." Abdirahman exited the specially designed language classroom at the end of his 2nd-grade year.

Our data show that beginning in late 1st grade and through his 3rd-grade year Abdirahman continued to excel in his reading, writing, and oral language proficiency. Abdirahman maintained his positive outlook on school, although he began to articulate that some things in school were hard for him. In 5th grade, in relation to writing, he explained, "Sometimes writing is hard for me. I think of too many good topics and I can't pick what to write about it." A small flattening of reading achievement occurred for Abdirahman in 3rd grade, but overall his literacy skills made steady growth toward grade-level norms, and by the end of 6th grade he was reading above grade level.

In 4th grade Abdirahman moved to a local K–12 charter school. During his 3 years at this school, he did not receive reading intervention support or systematic small-group instruction. Abdirahman had learned much about school behavior by 5th grade and had developed oral language skills that supported his academic literacy. For example, after attending an environmental fieldtrip on a boat that conducted science experiments involving the local river, he drew a picture of the boat with his classmates aboard. He labeled the on-ship laboratories and wrote a sentence explaining what he had experienced (see Figure 3.1).

Figure 3.1. Abdirahman's 5th-Grade Writing Sample

I am in 5th grade mr. Pajak used
to be my home room but we
switched to mc linner. we went to
mississippi River in fith grade.
We learned about insects that
live in mississippi and I saw
a bald eagle.

insect lab
labotary

secret la botr-for
captin

Despite these basic written sentences, a conversation with Abdirahman revealed much more about his new understandings. In response to, "Tell me more about that," he spoke about the connection between the river and the local environment. He said, "Do you know . . . do you know that holes over there . . . like the drains on the sidewalk. Whatever goes in there goes all the way in there with trash and gets out to the river." Although he struggled to come up with the precise words in English for *sewer grates*, he conveyed meaning through his description. This was a common characteristic of Abdirahman's language development. He was persistent about making sure that his audience understood him. And yet, although comprehensible, neither his oral nor written language exhibited the characteristics of academic English we hope students are able to use at the intermediate level.

Abdirahman had not yet acquired specialized vocabulary, knowledge of complex sentence structures, or understandings of how paragraphs, sentences, and text features work together. This appears to be typical of many emergent bilinguals in elementary schools, who may spend years learning conversational, everyday English, but for whom describing their thinking with extended and connected discourse is difficult. In later elementary years, our observations of Abdirahman reveal a more mature and restrained student who persists at language and literacy tasks while still maintaining some of his innate gregarious characteristics. In his 5th-grade classroom we observed him working independently on writing a poem, "I Am a Winner." He was focused on his work, writing a final draft of the poem even though kids around him were talking about their work or goofing around. Abdirahman kept focused on his writing, sounding out words aloud as he composed. He pondered over what word to use for his poem. Suddenly, Abdirahman looked up and exclaimed with pride, "Done!"

Chue

Like many of the children we met in this journey, Chue's 1st- and 2nd-grade years were spent in the Language Academy classroom for newcomer students. During 1st and 2nd grade, when we observed Chue, he was generally quiet and not engaged in large-group activities. In small-group or independent time he often worked alone or with a particular group of Hmong boys. We did not often observe him speaking, but when he did, it was almost exclusively in Hmong or in one-word sentences like "mine" and "okay." He typically used nonverbal cues, such as pointing, to express what he needed. By the end of 2nd grade, Chue started to form compound sentences using present tense verbs, such as, "His father he is coming to eat and play the guitar," and, "When I go to the market I buy a food and apple and banana." (See Figure 3.2.)

Figure 3.2. Chue's Writing Sample

Third- and 4th-grade observations showed Chue using much longer sentences and a variety of verb tenses, yet still making significant errors in sentences, such as this one: "When he do his homework, he fell asleep then he woke up he say he don't want to, don't need to do his homework, the computer already do to her." Besides verb agreement, he was still having difficulty with pronouns, and his vocabulary was limited to common words. In our final observations of Chue's English language in 6th grade, he produced longer and more complex sentences using some academic vocabulary, such as "hurricane," "t-rex," and "classmate." He used English to participate in academic tasks in whole-group and small-group situations, yet switched to Hmong when speaking individually to Hmong friends in class or on the playground. His 6th-grade ELL teacher commented:

> When I observe him socially, he sticks to Hmong. He is very engaged with his Hmong peers, he gets loud, he is outspoken. His confidence is low in using academic English, for obvious reasons. Six years is not long enough to master it, but he is definitely not lost when it comes to academics and he demonstrates his ability to be engaged and on topic.

Chue's elementary teachers' overall sense of him was that he was savvy socially, but not academically. In general, many teachers didn't seem to be worried about Chue's academic progress, although he continued to perform below grade-level expectations. As he left elementary school, his teachers described him as a confident student with the skills necessary to persist even though his reading levels were many years below grade level.

Diverging Paths

As we worked with these two boys over the years, we began to see ways in which their language and literacy development differed. By the end of 6th grade, the gap between these two learners was equal to several years. We began to wonder: *Why do two English learners who start with similar language and literacy skills end up at such different places?* A close look at the first years of Abdirahman's and Chue's language development reveals some of the origins of the gap and highlights factors that may explain the disparity.

Abdirahman and Chue began their elementary schooling with virtually the same level of proficiency in oral English. Figure 3.3 shows the boys' scores on an assessment of receptive and productive English (De Avila & Duncan, 1994) given twice a year from 1st through 3rd grades. They both scored in the range of "non-English speaker" in the fall of 1st grade with nearly equivalent raw scores. At this time, the boys were able to use some basic English words and could put them together in short phrases to communicate simple ideas and needs.

Figure 3.3. Oral Language Assessment Scores for Chue and Abdirahman

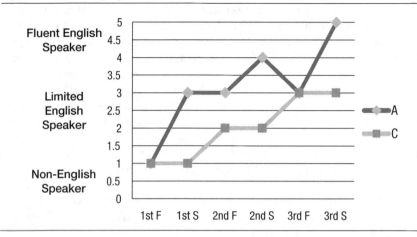

By the end of 3rd grade, their language levels had increased, although not in a smooth trajectory. Abdirahman's scores had increased rapidly, gaining 54 points across 3 years and reaching the top of the scale. In contrast, by the end of 3rd grade, Chue scored only 36 points higher than when he was first assessed and was still at level 3 ("limited English speaker"). Although he was not given this assessment after 3rd grade, in 5th grade on an assessment of productive vocabulary (Dunn & Dunn, 2007), Chue's score was equivalent to the norm for an English-speaking kindergarten student. His was the lowest language score among the students with whom we worked.

We know that language and literacy are tightly linked. Research highlights the positive correlation between English language development and reading achievement, and the inverse also holds true: Low levels of English language development are associated with low reading achievement (Lesaux & Geva, 2006; Saunders & O'Brien, 2006). Language skills in English are a necessary foundation for reading and comprehending English texts, and yet language and literacy develop in a way that is dynamic and reciprocal. Rather than a student acquiring oral English and then adding literacy, the two grow simultaneously. When children's English language is stronger, they comprehend better. And the more they read, the more English they learn. This synergistic growth allows students to access, use, and create increasingly complex and academic language in schools. As teachers, we have seen many students "take off" in language and literacy, and others who seemed to plateau or even "sink" in their language and literacy use. A look at Abdirahman's and Chue's reading proficiency across grades reveals the language–literacy relationship.

Figure 3.4 presents the approximate reading levels of Abdirahman and Chue in the fall and spring of each grade as assessed on informal reading inventories twice per year. Again, both boys started 1st grade at the

Figure 3.4. Chue's and Abdirahman's Reading Levels in 1st Through 6th Grades

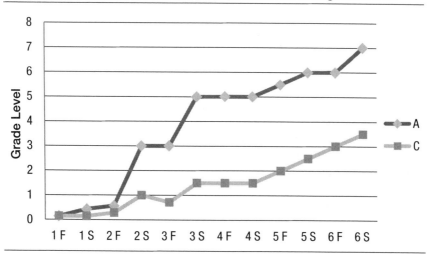

same reading level, about a year behind their grade-level peers. In 1st grade, they slowly gained foundational literacy skills like concept of word and the alphabetic principle, while also growing their English vocabulary. By the end of 2nd grade, however, their trajectories took widely different turns. Although both students' literacy skills were growing, Abdirahman made an enormous leap in 2nd grade and was reading at or above grade level each year beyond that. Chue's reading level advanced much more slowly. Although he made progress toward grade-level literacy skills in 2nd grade, a "summer slump" caused him to fall behind his previous progress at the beginning of 3rd grade. From 3rd grade on, Chue remained two to three grade levels behind in his reading. This means that not only was he unable to attain grade-level benchmarks, but he actually got further and further behind with passing time. By the end of 6th grade, his reading was almost 3 years below grade level.

Figure 3.5 shows examples of Chue's and Abdirahman's developmental spelling in the spring of 6th grade. Each student was given a qualitative spelling inventory designed to best assess his understanding of the English writing system. Chue was given the Elementary Spelling Inventory, and Abdirahman was given the Upper Level Spelling Inventory (Bear, Invernizzi, Templeton, & Johnston, 2012). Qualitative spelling inventories highlight a student's understanding of the ways that letters, letter patterns, and word parts work in the English language. By the end of 6th grade, students typically reach the advanced stage called *derivational relations* at which they are able to understand and use the spelling features in words to ascertain their meaning, such as understanding that the prefix "dis-" in the word *disloyal* means "not." In 6th grade, Abdirahman was working with words at this level; however, Chue was many levels behind. His spelling inventory reveals a continued confusion with short vowel sounds, blends, and other spelling patterns in English. This level is more typical of a 2nd- or 3rd-grade native English-speaking student.

While these data provide only snapshots of the boys' academic growth, they do represent a larger pattern in their development. Examined together, these data point out the linked nature of language, literacy, and overall academic achievement. For Abdirahman, language and literacy proficiency seemed to feed each other and accelerate his growth over time. His strong oral English skills appeared to both add to and grow from his speedy acquisition of literacy in English. Chue's slower acquisition of English language proficiency, coupled with his struggles to gain foundational literacy skills, led to a more problematic path. It appears that Chue's lower language skills created a constraint that weighed down his overall progress in literacy. Although he showed positive effort in his classes, he struggled in all academic areas and left elementary school years behind his peers.

Figure 3.5. Sample 6th-Grade Spelling Errors

Elementary Spelling Inventory 6th Grade, Spring 2012 Chue	Upper-Level Spelling Inventory 6th Grade, Spring 2012 Abdirahman
1. bed	1. swich
2. ship	2. smudge
3. when	3. tcalled
4. lomp	4. scrape
5. float	5. notted
6. train	6. shaving
7. place	7. squirt
8. drive	8. pounce
9. brite	9. scrathes
10. shopping	10. cratepcrater
11. slow	11. sailor
12. saving	12. village
13. chowed	13. disloyal

As you learned in Chapter 2, often the resources children bring to school are not well matched to school expectations; however, research has demonstrated that there are ways to sustain and accelerate the development of language in academic settings. The school-level supports and instruction that students and their families receive can make a tremendous difference to their academic success. One of the ways that educators can effect a positive change for students is to keep a keen eye on developing academic language throughout their school years.

As we reflect on the academic journeys of Chue and Abdirahman, we believe that academic language proficiency (or lack thereof) is one of the central differences in the boys' experiences. Although Chue could maintain a friendly conversation and participated in class, his limited academic English skills held him back in his coursework. For example, in his 6th-grade reading journal, he was asked to consider the author's message in a book he had read. The teacher had scaffolded the response by providing an academic language prompt: *I believe that the author is trying to say_____.* Although the prompt helped him to formulate a response, he was not able to demonstrate his comprehension of the text or the author's message. He wrote, "I believe that the author is trying to say there are having fun because sometime ceremonial was fun." Chue's interpretation of the author's meaning revolved around a surface-level impression of the content. Lack of academic language proficiency impeded his acquisition of new knowledge and his ability to express what he did understand. It is unfortunate yet predictable that language will be a barrier to Chue's future academic success. In the next section we share ways that teachers can intentionally support students' academic language learning.

THE TEACHER'S ROLE IN PROMOTING ACADEMIC LANGUAGE GROWTH

The good news is that educators can make a difference for students by making academic language part of their teaching. Teachers play a significant role in the development of children's academic language by ensuring that during the hours students spend in school, they are immersed in a fruitful environment for English learning. Language teaching happens both through explicit teaching and through environmental support, and teachers should be mindful of both pathways. Environmental language teaching involves creating rich and varied language settings and activities for students to engage in and practice communicating in English. Explicit language teaching is based in formative assessment and focused instruction for students with a specific language objective in mind. Recall Abdirahman's fieldtrip. He was exposed to language, such as *laboratory,* and complex ideas about the relationship between the river and the sewer grates, but lacked the explicit instruction in how to render those ideas in writing and speaking. A teacher might draw out more complex ideas from a student such as Abdirahman by creating a set of sentence stems to build off and guiding students to work in partnerships to practice using the sentences prior to doing their writing.

Over the 6 years we followed the students in this book, we encountered many talented and knowledgeable teachers who were adept at promoting language in their classrooms. Here we outline four key strategies that we observed that all teachers can use to help their English-learning students excel.

Modifying Your Own Language

The language that teachers use in school is important. Sometimes teachers focus their attention on objectives, activities, and routines, yet they forget to consider *how* information is presented to students. As the most significant model of fluent English speaking in many emergent bilinguals' lives, teachers must examine and modify the language they use in the classroom. There are two important considerations when thinking about teacher language to support emergent bilinguals.

First, the language used in the classroom needs to be comprehensible to students. Teachers should use words, phrases, sentence structures, and idioms that are familiar to students. Instead of talking in lengthy stretches or giving wordy instructions, teachers can reduce the linguistic density for students by rephrasing, using visuals, and generally speaking less so that English learners do not become overwhelmed by the flow of oral language.

Additionally, it is important for teachers to consider how to model the use of accurate, precise, and varied language to express ideas. Just as teachers ask students to banish the use of words like *stuff* and *things* and *like* because they are overused and not precise, teachers need to ensure that they are demonstrating the use of academic language. Teachers can use academic language throughout the day, especially in giving directions, while thinking aloud, during class discussions, and in shared writing activities. In combination with the first point—that language needs to be comprehensible to students—this becomes quite challenging. Yet, a focus on the use of comprehensible academic language in the classroom stands to make a big difference for English-learning students.

Connecting to Students' Home Languages

Sometimes, teachers who don't share their students' first language(s) feel uneasy about allowing the use of these languages in the classroom. Unknowingly, these teachers are cutting off a valuable learning resource for students by discouraging them from making connections between their home language and English. Several studies have demonstrated the importance of building on children's first language as a resource for developing English proficiency (Collier & Thomas, 2004; Genesee, Lindholm-Leary, Saunders, & Christian, 2006). In the classroom teachers can help emergent bilinguals take advantage of the language skills developed in their first language as a bridge to new skills in English.

One way that teachers can tap into their students' home language resources is by strategically using cognates—words that have the same linguistic origin and thus similar spellings and meanings—to develop students' reading comprehension in English. Helping students to notice these words while reading together or discussing academic content can lead to the ability to notice how similar (and different) meanings and spelling patterns show up in words. If teachers are unable to access cognates themselves, they can invite students to become aware of them by encouraging discussion with other students who speak their language. For example, in 3rd grade when Chue was unable to come up with the English word for *fishing line*, his teacher linked to his background knowledge, since she knew that he and his family often went fishing. "I want you to think about when you go fishing with your family. What are the things you need to bring with you?" The teacher allowed him some time to think and then prompted, "Say the word in Hmong before saying it in English." Chue's teacher challenged him to make connections between his native language, personal experiences, and English through these types of activities. The teacher's question was a good first step. To ensure that the connection carried over into Chue's academic language learning, she could follow up by having him record his new vocabulary in a personal notebook with illustrations, use the new words in a structured writing assignment, or add the new words to a vocabulary chart posted in the classroom for his reference.

There is also evidence that students who develop literacy skills in their first language are able to transfer many of those skills to English (Francis, Lesaux, & August, 2006; Slavin & Cheung, 2005). Proficiency in first-language literacy is related to English word reading, reading comprehension, reading strategies, spelling, and writing. Teachers and other school staff members play an important role in encouraging children and their families to continue to speak, read, and write in their first language as they are learning English in schools. This is a particularly important message for parents who may have the mistaken understanding that the best way to support their child's English development is by discontinuing the use of their first language in their home. Teachers need to let family members know that helping their children develop in the home language also will help them progress in English. Playing games, singing songs, telling stories, writing letters to relatives, and discussing current events are examples of activities that families can engage in to help their children expand the vocabulary and syntax of their first language while learning a new one. New words in English may connect to ideas and labels that students already have in their home language. Having a strong academic language base in their first language will support students' acquisition and concept development in the new language.

Making Classroom Interaction a Priority

English learners who are instructed primarily using "sit and get" approaches, where the teacher talks and students listen, often become disengaged in lessons due to the cognitive overload of constantly trying to comprehend in a new language and not being held accountable to use it. Instead, teachers can facilitate active construction of knowledge in which students are involved in their own learning and are using language to process new information. Chue's 1st-grade teacher made a point of including verbal interaction in nearly all of her lessons. For example, when she worked with small reading groups, she asked, "Chue, what do you think? If you don't know, ask your friends." She wanted him to practice speaking English with peers and help him to develop strategies for learning unknown words. This was an important first step to encourage Chue to use classroom language. It is also critical that he receive models of increasingly complex academic language, as discussed next.

Teaching Academic Vocabulary and Language

All teachers need to be language and literacy teachers as well as teachers of their content areas because all content learning is mediated by oral and written language. In elementary classrooms, language instruction should be incorporated in lessons throughout the day in order for students to understand the content of the lesson and also to add new English words and structures to their **lexicons**. For example, one day when we visited Abdirahman's 1st-grade class, the teacher was engaging students in an interactive read-aloud of the story *The Little Old Lady Who Was Not Afraid of Anything* (Williams, Roberts, Roberts, & Corrigan, 1986). All of the students sat on the carpet in front of the big book as she read. Then, during a second read, the teacher asked volunteers to play different parts of the book: pants, shirts, boots, hat, pumpkin head, and the old lady. As the volunteers acted out their parts, the rest of the group participated by repeating aloud and acting out words, such as *wiggle, wiggle* and *clomp, clomp*. In this way, Abdirahman's teacher wove language instruction throughout her literacy lesson by including repetition, chanting, and movements.

One way to focus on teaching language is to incorporate **academic language objectives** for each lesson, whether in reading, math, music, or another discipline. An academic language objective can focus on teaching a new word or group of words, a sentence structure, or how to communicate across different contexts. For example, in a reading lesson in which students are comparing and contrasting character traits, the language objectives might focus on the language of comparison ("The characters are *similar* because . . . "), on a particularly challenging sentence structure from the text, or on specific vocabulary words and their meanings. By focusing on language, teaching its usage, and allowing students to practice, all teachers can help emergent bilinguals to grow.

When planning academic language instruction, teachers may want to follow a four-step process of determining objectives that meet students' needs, and then teaching and assessing them. Figure 3.6 shows this process.

1. Assess language use. Teachers need to be acutely aware of the language that is being used in their classrooms. By becoming careful listeners of students' oral language and conscientious examiners of students' written

Figure 3.6. Four-Step Process for Planning Language Objectives

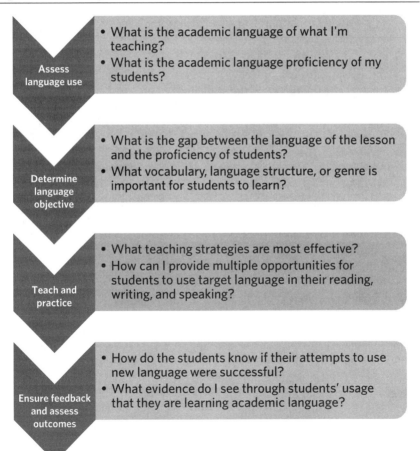

Assess language use
- What is the academic language of what I'm teaching?
- What is the academic language proficiency of my students?

Determine language objective
- What is the gap between the language of the lesson and the proficiency of students?
- What vocabulary, language structure, or genre is important for students to learn?

Teach and practice
- What teaching strategies are most effective?
- How can I provide multiple opportunities for students to use target language in their reading, writing, and speaking?

Ensure feedback and assess outcomes
- How do the students know if their attempts to use new language were successful?
- What evidence do I see through students' usage that they are learning academic language?

language, teachers can gather useful data about the words, syntax, and discourse that their students are or are not using. Of course, teachers listen to students speaking in class every day, but they usually "tune in" to the message or what it is that the student is communicating. Here, we advocate switching gears to listen for *how* a student is communicating the message. Chue's 3rd-grade teacher made assessing language part of her regular practice: "I do observations throughout the day, orally having conversations with students. It tells me a lot, having conversations with them, talking about books. I really rely on what I know about my kids and how much time I spend talking to them."

Making language information gathering part of teaching practice means asking questions like:

- Is the student successfully communicating her or his message? Can she/he be understood by classmates and teachers?
- What words does the student use repeatedly? And what words does she/he leave out or dance around, using longer or less precise language?
- Does the student use prepositional phrases correctly?
- How is her/his grammar? Which grammatical structures are incorrect or avoided by the student?
- Does the student's language convey the correct level of formality or does it sound as if she/he is speaking to a buddy when answering questions in class?

Many teachers find it useful to keep records of their observations of students' language in order to retain information that they otherwise might forget during the busy school day. Having a system for informal note-taking at the ready makes data collection quick and easy. This may involve using a handy clipboard with a sheet or note card for each child or an electronic tablet with a note-taking app. Teachers also can use checklists or rubrics to record observations of particular aspects of student language performance. These records can provide useful information to help teachers bridge the gap between the academic language used in class and the language used by students.

Once teachers become more aware of the language needs of their students, they are able to provide the focused instruction and scaffolding needed to improve language and content learning. After 3rd grade, Chue's and Abdirahman's language development took divergent paths. In retrospect, perhaps a more careful analysis of Chue's written language and observational data could have brought to light the particular words and language forms he was "using but confusing" so that he could have been given special support. Although it's not practical to ask teachers to provide personalized language instruction for each student, this kind of information gathering could help teachers see patterns across many of their emergent bilingual students, to be addressed in small groups or with differentiated learning activities.

2. Determine language objectives. In addition to knowing the language of their students, teachers should know the language of their curriculum. By curriculum, we are referring to the written texts used in class as well as the verbal text of lessons, lectures, and discussions. A close look at these classroom texts through the lens of language reveals specific words, conventions, and structures that could cause difficulties for students. Finding tricky vocabulary words is one piece of the puzzle that is commonly part of teachers' practice, and yet this is not enough for students who are learning academic English. Teachers also must consider how multiple words are put together into phrases and sentences, as this is often where students encounter difficulty. Consider the following excerpt from *The American Vision* (Appleby, Brinkley, McPherson, & Broussard, 2003), a U.S. history textbook:

> These concerns were an important reason why many people, including merchants, artisans, and creditors, began to argue for a strong central government, and several members of the Confederation Congress called on the states to correct "such defects as may be discovered to exist" in the present government. (p. 161)

It is not only the words that will cause students difficulties with this passage, but also the number of meaning units (clauses) put together into one sentence. It is easy to lose track of the author's meaning by the end of the sentence. By looking for what makes a passage complex in classroom texts, teachers can preteach and practice such language structures to increase comprehension and encourage students' production of more complex language. Teaching students to dissect and comprehend complex sentences, such as the example above, constitutes a language objective for the lesson.

To demonstrate how a teacher might do this, we call upon "A Vision of Explicit Language Instruction" developed by Susana Dutro (Dutro et al., 2016). After teachers have collected informal assessment data from their students and examined the text that students will work with, they should: (a) consider the specific vocabulary words or phrases that are needed to understand the text, and (b) identify the sentence structures and grammatical features that are used for that particular communication purpose. In the example above from the history text, a key sentence structure would likely be: "These *concerns* were an important reason why many people, including *merchants, artisans, and creditors,* began to *argue for a strong central government* . . . ." This chunk of the sentence could be used as a frame to create other complex sentences by substituting in different academic vocabulary for the italicized words, such as, "These *incidents* were an important reason why many people, including *drivers, bicycle riders, and pedestrians,* began to *call for better bike paths in the city.*"

3. Teach and practice. Noticing the language used by students and examining the language used in classroom texts are two important steps in becoming a teacher of academic language; the next step is to work to connect the two through focused instruction and opportunities for practice.

There are many strategies for teaching academic language across the content areas in elementary school. An example is a sentence frame that scaffolds new language structures by providing written models on a sentence strip, table tent, or interactive whiteboard. For example, when asking students to make inferences from their reading, provide the frame, "Based on _____, I infer _____ because _____." Also, teachers need to make *looking closely at* and *talking about* how words are used part of the everyday practice of the classroom. Allow time for students to share interesting words they've heard and read as well as those they have questions about. Another idea is to provide content texts in an informal register and have students translate these to academic language, and vice versa. The key is to think in terms of unlocking the academic register in order to let the students in on the secret. By being explicit about the features of academic language and its use, teachers help students decipher the hidden language of texts.

4. Ensure feedback and assess outcomes. As with all learning objectives, teachers should assess whether their students are meeting academic language objectives. Formative assessments based on teachers' observations of student presentations and analysis of written products can be seamlessly embedded in everyday tasks. It's important not to restrict authentic, everyday language in the classroom in an effort to focus on academic language. Students use everyday language to collaborate and process ideas, and this should not be thwarted but encouraged. Even as they interact informally, stretch students to include specific academic vocabulary and language structures that are listed on classroom charts and vocabulary walls. Remember that the goal is for students to know and use academic language when it's called for—being able to strategically switch from informal to formal registers.

Feedback is an important aspect of language learning. Teachers can help students to understand how to use and comprehend complex language through brief, timely comments or written feedback. Commending students for the turn of a phrase or the use of a word that makes them sound like an author is a great way to affirm their efforts; however, correcting errors may cause unwanted attention or embarrassment, so do so without putting students on the spot, especially in front of others.

The academic language planning cycle begins anew as information from observations of students, along with the grade-level standards, informs teachers where to focus linguistic instruction. The process of examining classroom texts for complex academic language also continues. As teachers gain confidence with this process, using a language lens to evaluate classroom materials will become second nature. Becoming a teacher of academic language requires changing perspectives and practices so that instruction is responsive to the language students bring to school with them.

SUMMARIZING LEARNING

As we look back and reflect on Chue's and Abdirahman's elementary school years, we are struck by how two boys who received very similar educational inputs (school, program structure, literacy curriculum, and teachers) can have such dissimilar outcomes. We postulate that the acquisition of academic English played a substantial role in the boys' educational performance. By 3rd grade, the differences between the ways the two students used English became evident. Although we can't determine *why* one of the students was more successful at language learning than the other, we can use these data to examine the complexity of interacting factors at work. The boys had different home languages—could one language be more similar to English and therefore be "easier" to transfer? The boys had different preschool experiences—could exposure to language and literacy at a young age make a difference in school? The boys had different personality types; Abdirahman was outgoing and physically active, while Chue was quiet and independent. Could these characteristics have made a difference in how actively they practiced and learned English? And, although they had very similar school experiences, they did have several different teachers along the way. Could some of their teachers have been more effective at assessing and teaching academic English? By looking closely at these two boys' experiences, we have renewed our own beliefs that supporting emergent bilinguals in schools cannot happen with a one-size-fits-all intervention; rather, it takes teachers knowing their students, knowing the academic language of their curriculum, and knowing how to teach it.

In this chapter perhaps you discovered that you are (or will be) the most significant model of fluent English language with whom your students engage, and have become aware of how important your use of precise and academic language is to your students' language development. We hope that you will now view your multilingual classroom through a "language lens" when planning daily instruction. This language lens will help you to see and know your students' use of language as well as the language demands of the curriculum.

QUESTIONS FOR REFLECTION AND DISCUSSION

- The title of this chapter is Learning Academic Language. What have you learned about academic language and its importance? How are literacy and academic language development related?
- Think about your classroom or a classroom you've been in. How is language taught? Is it environmentally supported or explicit? What is your evidence?
- Review, reflect on, and discuss the possible strategies a teacher might implement during language instruction with emergent bilinguals. Have you used these strategies, or what ideas did you glean for trying out something new?
- What is sticking with you from the chapter? How do the students you work with seem similar to Abdirahman and Chue?

CHAPTER 4

Creating Strong Relationships with Students

A MOMENT BETWEEN MS. LANSING AND CHUE

It is late October and the 1st-grade students in Ms. Lansing's Language Academy classroom are huddled around two big tables working on an art project for Halloween. Chue reaches into a scattered pile of markers and crayons that are spread across the table and grabs an orange crayon. He begins to color in the head of his drawing of a pumpkin-faced scarecrow. He is chatting vigorously in Hmong with two other boys sitting next to him. Ms. Lansing and a volunteer from a local university circulate around the room and frequently stop to talk to students about their work. Ms. Lansing gravitates over to Chue and the two boys he is working with. Ms. Lansing is White and does not speak Hmong. She points to a poster in the classroom displaying the sight words, "I can see . . . " written in big letters. Motioning to Chue's drawing, she slowly utters, "I can see a pumpkin." Chue grins and points down to the orange crayon scribbles on his page that outline a lop-sided head of a scarecrow and hesitantly articulates the word "pumpkin" in English. Ms. Lansing pauses and gestures for the volunteer, who speaks Hmong, to come over and asks her to translate what the students are talking about. The volunteer listens for a moment and then describes how the students are telling one another monster stories from the Hmong culture. The students were reminded of these stories by the image of the pumpkin-headed scarecrow. Additionally, the students are complimenting one another's artwork as they work.

A few weeks after this lesson, Ms. Lansing reflected on this exchange with Lori and Carrie. She described how this moment had struck her. Ms. Lansing felt concerned and overwhelmed about the language gap between her and her students. She pondered what this meant in terms of *knowing* them. "I feel like I know my students, but you don't really know them because there is this whole other level that you can't access because you don't speak their language and I never think about what their chattering is about." Ms. Lansing continued, "It's something I think I never thought about because I never actually hear regular conversation because anytime I can understand them it is very limited with their vocabulary. . . . I guess it is just I never really thought about what a 6-year-old kid would be talking about as they are coloring in the scary pumpkin head." Ms. Lansing's words reflect the key dilemma in this chapter: How do you build relationships with students and their families when you don't speak their home language or come from the same cultural or discourse communities that they do?

For many educators, the desire to become a teacher is grounded in a passion for working with children. Often, students in teacher education programs attribute their motivation to become a teacher to a previous significant experience working with kids or to a noteworthy relationship they had with a teacher when they were going through school. If you think back on your own personal experiences in school, you probably remember a time that a relationship you had with a teacher influenced you in a positive way. Observing individuals over the course of 6 years taught us a lot about the role of relationships in student success at school. The students had different linguistic and cultural backgrounds, shy or outgoing personalities, and unique interests. Their teachers, the majority of whom were White and native English speakers, interacted with the children in a variety of ways—and students showed greater engagement and motivation at school when teachers made connections to their identities and interests. Throughout this chapter we describe ways that teachers we observed attempted to put getting to know their students at the forefront of their teaching. We grapple with how to build meaningful and supportive relationships with students and their families while making teaching and learning relevant to the languages, literacies, and cultural practices of multilingual students.

> **Essential Dilemma:** How do you build relationships with students and their families when you don't speak their home language or come from the same cultural or discourse communities as they do?
>
> Individuals are a part of multiple discourse communities. Discourse refers to the ways people use language, gain understanding, and act in order to be recognized socially by members of a community (Gee, 2014). Discourse communities form the ways we come to understand things and shape what we call our identity.
>
> Examples of discourse communities include elementary education teacher, Spanish speaker, female/male, White, and middle class.

THE IMPORTANCE OF RELATIONSHIPS

Positive relationships between multilingual students and their teachers are linked to academic engagement and success in school (Chhuon & Wallace,

2012; Cummins, 2000; Jiménez & Rose, 2010; Ladson-Billings, 1995; Valdés, 2001; Valenzuela, 1999). Identity markers such as race, language, gender, and social class are always a piece of the relational puzzle—adding to the dynamic and ever-evolving teacher–student relational process (Jiménez, 2000). Forging authentic relationships with students is never a simple task, and adding to the complexity of the task are larger sociopolitical factors, such as current educational reform initiatives, nationwide population shifts toward a majority multilingual society, and the **demographic divide**, the demographic disparities between the student and teacher populations in the United States.

Given this reality, many educational researchers and teachers continue to work together to define and share teaching practices and pedagogies that support linguistically diverse students' academic achievement in the classroom and recognize the cultural and linguistic communities from which they come (Jiménez & Rose, 2010; Ladson-Billings, 1995; Moll, Amanti, Neff, & Gonzalez, 1992; Paris, 2012; Paris & Alim, 2014). An approach that you learned about in Chapter 2 that aligns with this research highlights the different cultural, linguistic, and sociological funds of knowledge that exist in students' home communities (Moll et al., 1992). When teachers build upon students' funds of knowledge, there is the potential to forge stronger relationships of openness and trust.

Let's look back to the moment between Ms. Lansing and Chue. What made Ms. Lansing want to know what the students were talking about in Hmong on this particular day? What inspired her to ask her volunteer to interpret what the students were saying? And, how did it help her think differently about her students? These are important questions to address for teachers of multilingual students. Although we don't know the answers to all of these questions, what we do know is that Ms. Lansing's co-teacher was gone for the day and she had planned a low-key art activity for her students that did not demand too much instructional support from her. So, during the lesson, she didn't feel as much pressure and could interact more with the students. We know the lesson happened on a day before a holiday—which in schools are typically days that are more relaxed. Most important, we know that this lesson created an opening for Ms. Lansing to stop and notice her students in ways that she hadn't before. From this simple interaction, Ms. Lansing *knew* her students better. She now knew that Chue was making connections between the lesson and his own culture, and that his peers supported him through complimenting his artwork. This is just one tiny example of how teachers can leverage their students' strengths and use cultural resources to enhance English literacy instruction and build relationships every day.

To understand more about how the teachers we observed attempted to build strong, supportive relationships with their students, we explore three *ways of knowing* that teachers can draw upon to get to know students and support them academically. These three ways of knowing are: moving beyond "just teach" teacher relationships; providing **instrumental support**; and engaging in a "benefit-of-the-doubt" treatment of students (Chhuon & Wallace, 2012). As we define and discuss each of the ways of knowing, keep in mind that these ideas can help educators to think about building strong relationships with transnational and multilingual students. They do not, however, provide a checklist for cultural competency. Instead, they offer possibilities for educators to think about relationship building with students through an approach that Rosalie Rolón-Dow (2005) calls *critical care*, taking into consideration the broader sociopolitical context.

Below, we take a deeper look into these three ways of knowing, through highlighting the relationships between specific teachers and students in this project.

Moving Beyond "Just Teach" Teacher Relationships—
Ms. Jacobson and Tong

It is the beginning of the literacy block in Ms. Jacobson's 5th-grade classroom at Randolph Elementary. The diverse group of 28 students has just finished the daily morning meeting and are shuffling around the room gathering their literacy materials and getting into guided-reading groups at one of six rectangular tables. The classroom is brightly lit and feels warm as the ice continues to form on the outside of the windows during this short month of February. At the front of the room, Ms. Jacobson picks up a big flipchart with the title, "Let's Talk About It," in bold green letters on the cover and props it up on an easel. This flipchart is a part of the schoolwide literacy curriculum and is filled with engaging full-color photos that promote conversation and oral language development for students learning English. As the title of the flipchart suggests, the purpose of these large photos is to encourage students to explore and share their understandings of the world around them through talk (Mondo Educational Publishing, 2015).

Ms. Jacobson plops down on the floor next to the easel. She calls out over the low buzz of students' voices for the Blue Group to come join her on the carpet. Tong, along with three other Hmong students and one Somali student, heads toward the carpet. Ms. Jacobson greets the students by name and takes the time to ask each student how they are doing. Observing this interaction, Maggie notices a big smile stretch across Tong's face as he sits down close to Ms. Jacobson in the semicircle. He takes a deep breath, sighs, and appears content to be participating in this small-group activity with his teacher. Tong is often silent in large-group discussions. However, his demeanor as a student changes in small-group settings. Ms. Jacobson is aware of this and provides multiple opportunities for Tong to participate in these smaller group interactions.

Ms. Jacobson explains the purpose of the lesson to the students, describing how they will use the photo as "an anchor" for their discussion. Silently, the students and Ms. Jacobson take a moment to absorb the details of the photo. The flipchart is open to a photo of a young boy, with brown-colored skin and short brown hair, lying on a twin-sized bed in a small bedroom. Tong is looking intently at the picture. Ms. Jacobson pauses for a second and looks at Tong. "What are you thinking, Tong?" Tong takes a moment and then bursts out, "The boy is sleeping 'cause he probably played soccer really hard and is tired. The poster is probably his favorite poster . . . did I tell you I was playing soccer with my brother yesterday at the center?" Ms. Jacobson responds to Tong with a warm smile and a nod of her head. She reiterates Tong's response to the rest of the students, which initiates a group discussion about soccer. With his hands on his knees and his body leaning forward, Tong continues to share about his afternoon with his brother. Looking up at the clock, Ms. Jacobson gently interrupts Tong and reminds him that they have to move forward with the 15-minute lesson. She lets him know they can continue this conversation after the lesson.

Providing multilingual students with opportunities to talk about their ideas during instruction time is one way that Ms. Jacobson builds relationships with her students. Throughout the small-group lesson, Tong was actively articulating, communicating, and negotiating his ideas. Ms. Jacobson used multiple strategies to engage with Tong and move beyond a "just teach" stance, in which Ms. Jacobson would have acknowledged Tong's comment but immediately moved back into the predetermined topics and scripted prompt questions from the curriculum.

A major tension that teachers experience on a daily basis is time constraints because of pressures to cover content, school- or districtwide curriculum policies, a desire to include students' home and community resources into the lesson, and the student-to-teacher ratio, to name a few. Ms. Jacobson's decision to engage the students in a conversation about soccer could be viewed by her principal as veering away from the purpose of the lesson, or wasting "learning time." However, engaging her students in conversation about soccer did not waste instructional time. Ms. Jacobson's decision to engage the students in a conversation about soccer is an example of how she took Tong's interests and experiences and wove them into the lesson in a meaningful way. This happened not only through conversation during instructional time but also informally as they cleaned up after the lesson.

As the Blue Group's lesson comes to an end, Ms. Jacobson asks Tong to help her clean up the materials and put the easel back in the corner of the room. The two of them pause between tasks to chat about the lesson and Tong's time spent yesterday afternoon with his older brother. Ms. Jacobson asks Tong if the lesson got his "imagination rolling" for their current personal narrative writing project. Tong nods his head and continues to chat about soccer and his excitement for the spring season. He reflects on the lesson and shares that the boy's shoes in the photo remind him of his shoes and how in the winter when he gets home from school he takes off his shoes and puts them by the heater so they are warm for the next day. Ms. Jacobson reveals to Tong that the sport she likes to play is tennis. Tong talks faster and a bit louder as he tells a story about a time last summer when his older brother took him to play tennis. Tong inquires if they can play tennis together sometime. Grinning, Ms. Jacobson ends the conversation by stating, "Maybe some day in the spring at recess or during PE class we can play tennis together."

Ms. Jacobson knows that day-to-day interactions with students are essential. Using the students' names as they began the lesson, sitting on the floor with the students, and talking with Tong during clean-up—all of these small gestures—are integral to forming meaningful relationships between Ms. Jacobson and her students. While these may seem like simple, everyday components of teaching, the actions Ms. Jacobson took during the small-group oral language lesson were intentional. Just as Ms. Jacobson had to learn how to teach literacy methods, she also had to learn how to know her students. By moving beyond a "just teach" stance, Ms. Jacobson built trust with Tong, thereby increasing Tong's willingness to engage in learning and building mutual trust. Ms. Jacobson was able to implement practices that not only developed trust with Tong but also provided instrumental support to his academic success.

Throughout Tong's 5th-grade year, Ms. Jacobson moved beyond a "just teach" stance by actively taking initiative to care for her students on a personal level—by getting to know their identity and interests beyond the classroom walls. This bidirectional involvement between Ms. Jacobson and her students happened through lessons and conversations in the classroom and also by visiting her students in their homes or other places in the community, including after-school programs, the neighborhood public library, or students' extracurricular and sporting events.

Knowing that a student speaks Spanish with her parents at home, plays on a local Parks and Recreation soccer team, takes Arabic lessons at the community Mosque every Saturday, or cooks Ecuadorian meals with her grandmother on Thursday nights helps educators understand more about who their students are and where they come from. This knowledge can then be integrated into the literacy curriculum in meaningful ways. Table 4.1 offers several ideas for how to do this.

As the examples in Table 4.1 suggest, there are many ways to move beyond a "just teach" stance and use the sociocultural resources that multilingual students bring to the classroom to enhance their learning of

Table 4.1. Culturally Sustaining Teaching for the Common Core State Standards

Standard	Classroom Example
CCSS.ELA–LITERACY.W.1.2	
Write informative/explanatory texts in which they name a topic, supply some facts about the topic, and provide some sense of closure.	Students could author their own multilingual books using language and digital photographs from their home lives.
CCSS.MATH.2.10	
Draw a picture graph and a bar graph (with single-unit scale) to represent a data set with up to four categories. Solve simple put-together, take-apart, and compare problems using information presented in a bar graph.	Students could link family experiences to content areas in an interdisciplinary unit on transportation. Students could gather photos of types of transportation used by people in their family and could then create a graph and present their findings.
CCSS. ELA–LITERACY.W.3.6	
Conduct short research projects that build knowledge about a topic.	Students could conduct a mini oral history project about an individual or event in their family. The project could end with students creating some type of digital product that shares what they learned.

Source: NGA & CCSSO (2010).

standardized academic English. Ultimately, moving beyond a "just teach" stance means focusing on who students are, what they already do as literate beings, and how educators can use this information to engage students in powerful learning activities. We now turn to another teacher from the project, Mr. Starks, who epitomized numerous ways to provide structural, instructional, and relational support for students.

Providing Instrumental Support—Mr. Starks and Kevin

In the basement of an old brick charter school building, a group of 16 fifth-grade students, wearing the school uniform of khaki pants and maroon polo shirts, pushes through a narrow entryway into their homeroom on the way back from science class. The blue carpet on the floor is tattered in various places and opens up to a large classroom space. There are four rows of older wooden desks in the center of the room. To the right of the desks is an area with four small red-colored worktables. Six bookshelves filled with a combination of children's books, informational texts, and classroom materials are strategically placed around the room. A partition of wooden cubbies, filled with plastic containers housing literacy products that are clearly labeled for student use, borders the classroom library space that is filled with a variety of texts representing many different formats, content areas, and genres. To the left of the whiteboard, there is a word wall, posted at eye level for students to interact with. Displayed above the whiteboard are pendants from various U.S. colleges and universities. In between the pendants are positive affirmations such as, "Whether you think you can or you can't, you're right," and "Teamwork makes the dream work."

"No voices as we get ready, team. It needs to stay quiet as you get your materials for reading." As the teacher's voice gets louder, the chatter among the students entering the classroom diminishes. Although Mr. Starks is around 6 feet tall, he has a calming presence and quiet tone that rapidly gathers the attention of his students. Kevin whispers something quickly to a boy standing next to him and then silently grabs his reading materials from his cubby. Kevin sits down in the front row, faces forward, and gently places his hands on his reading book.

Kevin holds a great deal of respect for his 5th-grade teacher, Mr. Starks. They have developed a strong relationship built on mutual respect, care, and trust. Since his arrival from Mexico in 1st grade, Kevin has been in seven different classrooms in three different schools, and has had at least eight different teachers. Kevin's relationships with his teachers were not all equally strong. Some of his relationships with teachers were dynamic and ignited Kevin's passion for literacy, but others were rocky and had a negative effect on his engagement in school. Kevin's relationship with Mr. Starks was noticeably vibrant and particularly meaningful, and had an impact on his identity as a student and literacy learner. Throughout Kevin's 5th-grade year, Mr. Starks provided Kevin with support that impacted his literacy success in numerous ways. Below we explore some of the ways that Mr. Starks provided this instrumental support: by creating an engaging classroom environment and using consistent procedures and routines; by incorporating students' home languages into literacy lessons; and by cultivating a sense of connectedness.

Classroom design and consistency. The design of Mr. Starks's classroom and his consideration for the physical organization of materials and furniture contributed to the positive climate for his students. Mr. Starks took into consideration the positioning of both the individual student desks and the larger rectangular desks around the room so that he could accommodate different ways of interacting with groups and provide a variety of curricular activities for literacy content lessons. The varied curricula included both a schoolwide mandated direct instruction reading curriculum and Mr. Starks's self-generated interdisciplinary social studies curriculum that integrated balanced literacy and culturally relevant approaches. Mr. Starks made sure that the physical environment was conducive to the students' learning in different ways depending on the lesson. Often during their reading block, students worked in a whole group or individually at the rows of desks in the middle of the classroom. In this arrangement, all students faced Mr. Starks. He was in close proximity to them and there was enough space between the rows of desks for him to walk through and stop to work with individual students. Additionally, Mr. Starks created a seating arrangement that allowed students to communicate and work with partners (often in their home languages). He was intentional about where each student sat and who sat by whom.

Mr. Starks organized student materials so that his students had easy access. He posted materials on the classroom walls that supported the instructional and community resources and practices taken up by himself and his students. His classroom library was separated from the small-group working areas and was a quiet place where students went to read or work independently. Mr. Starks had more than one display area where student work was visible.

Another way that Mr. Starks provided instrumental support was through consistent routines. As illustrated in the vignette above, Kevin and the other students knew what to expect as they entered their homeroom after science class. Mr. Starks built trust with his students through his use of procedures and routines at the beginning, during, and at the end of lessons. For example, whenever students worked in small guided-reading groups, the lesson ended with students verbally summarizing what they had learned with the other students in their group. When routines and procedures are wisely taught, modeled, and recognized in the classroom, students know what's expected of them and how to complete classroom practices independently. Having these predictable patterns in place allowed Mr. Starks to spend more time engaging in meaningful **culturally sustaining** practices, which emphasize the pluralistic and evolving nature of multilingual students' identities, cultures, and literacy practices (Ladson-Billings, 1995; Paris, 2012; Paris & Alim, 2014).

> **Teaching Opportunity:** How does the design of your classroom and your consideration for the physical organization of materials and furniture contribute to a positive climate for your students?

Incorporating students' home languages into classroom instruction. Students from various sociolinguistic groups bring with them distinct experiences that shape their classroom understandings. Literacy goes beyond skillful processing of text—it involves comprehension and meaning-making that are mediated by one's social, cultural, and linguistic resources. Mr. Starks acknowledged and paid attention to the sociocultural resources that his students brought to the classroom every day. He knew that his students' language and literacy knowledge in English and their home languages influenced their identities and was intertwined with "the meaning and consequences of becoming and being literate" (Ferdman, 1990, p. 182). As he reiterated to Lori during an interview, he believed using students' home languages during literacy instruction not only helped his students "clarify what words meant but also helped them gain confidence in their own abilities in being multilingual." Several times, we observed him utilizing the home languages of his students to enhance their understanding of concepts and vocabulary words in English. For instance, in the vignette below, notice how Mr. Starks worked *with* his students to provide instrumental support toward their academic achievement in the lesson.

The group of 16 students collectively read the sentence, "I have confidence we can avoid a long conversation." Mr. Starks pauses after the reading and asks, "What word describes people talking to each other about something?" Most of the students, including Kevin, echo back, "conversation." There are a few students who do not respond. Maggie is observing this lesson and notices that Mr. Starks's eyes drift toward two Spanish-speaking students in the back row. He asks the class what the word for conversation is in Spanish. A few students, including Kevin, raise their hands to answer. Mr. Starks calls on one of the students from the back row. She quietly says, "la conversación." As soon as she says the word in Spanish, other students start to talk briefly in Spanish among themselves. Mr. Starks glances down at his watch and instructs the students to turn to a partner and talk briefly about what the word "conversation" means to them, using whatever language they want. Students turn their chairs and start discussing in English, Hmong, and Spanish with their partners.

In this excerpt, Mr. Starks demonstrated how to provide instrumental support by meshing the words and concepts that students use in their lives outside of the classroom and the standardized academic English they learned in school. Mr. Starks's integration of the Spanish language in literacy lessons appeared to impact Kevin's engagement in class in constructive ways—his learning increased, his grades went up, and he became more engrossed in reading and writing as his 5th-grade year progressed.

Kevin was one of 11 students in Mr. Starks's class who came from transnational families and received ELL services. This multilingual and multicultural reality was evident in the majority of the classrooms we observed throughout this project and reflects both national and global demographic trajectories. More people in the world move between multilingual settings in their day-to-day life than between monolingual settings. Present-day statistics estimate that more than half of the world's population uses two or more languages across family, school, and community communications (Grosjean, 2010; Paris & Alim, 2014). Kevin and the other multilingual students in Mr. Starks's class communicated in at least two different languages daily. Mr. Starks encouraged his students' language learning by thinking about ways to build upon, rather than ignore, their linguistic resources. This is a significant skill for educators of multilingual students to encourage.

Cultivating a sense of belonging. Kevin made significant academic gains during his 5th-grade year. For example, on the Measures of Academic Progress (MAP) test (Northwest Evaluation Association, 2011), Kevin's score went up 13 points, exceeding the five-point national annual growth average gain. What is more, his score on the 5th-grade state standardized reading test placed him in the "exceeds expectations" category. Although there are many factors that go into students' academic success each year, it is worth noting that Kevin made the most academic gains on literacy assessments during his 5th-grade year with Mr. Starks. We wonder whether the strong relationship between them could have been a factor in Kevin's success that year. In this final discussion about Mr. Starks and Kevin's relationship, we will explore the ways that Mr. Starks cultivated a sense of belonging with his students—and how this influenced Kevin in constructive ways.

Mr. Starks believed that the diversity found in his classroom strengthened student learning and he consistently created opportunities for conversations and constructive peer interactions. Mr. Starks exemplified this regularly not only through instruction but also through creating a sense of belonging so that his students felt comfortable taking risks and engaging in the work.

For example, during lessons Mr. Starks would name out loud the different ways that he observed students working hard. He made a point to provide positive encouragement to his students. He used sentences such as, "I have confidence that everyone will finish their reading work today," or, "Because we are a team, let's figure this one out together." He engaged with students' strengths during reading lessons to encourage them to use their creativity. This included drawing on Kevin's great sense of humor by choosing him to read the voice of a silly character. This gave Kevin an opportunity to make other students laugh, which he loved to do. Kevin was an active student, and other teachers saw his high energy as a deterrent to his successful learning. Despite this, Mr. Starks viewed Kevin's energy as a positive part of his personality. Mr. Starks used adjectives such as "energetic, eager, and smart," to describe Kevin and considered him a "good kid." During an interview with Lori, he shared, "He gets along well with others, he has a lot of energy, but it is interesting; I have not seen someone with as much energy as him love to sit down and read. He loves to sit down and open up a book. He is oblivious to the world when he does that; I think he has developed a love of reading." As observers in Mr. Starks's classroom during Kevin's 5th-grade year, it was apparent also to us that Kevin had developed a passion for reading and that it was woven together with the relationship he had with his teacher.

To this point in the chapter we have shared examples of teachers' building relationships with students. Below we explore the strategy of *engaging in a benefit-of-the-doubt treatment of students*, by moving to the following year to look closely at an example of disconnect between Kevin and his 6th-grade teacher, Ms. Smith.

Engaging in a Benefit-of-the-Doubt Treatment of Students— A Disconnect Between Ms. Smith and Kevin

It is late January and a group of students, including Kevin and 17 other 6th-graders, pile into Ms. Smith's language arts classroom. Maggie is observing in the back of the room. The students slowly and loudly make their way to the 18 desks. The desks are arranged in four rows in the middle of the room. Maggie has noticed Kevin's engagement and behavior in class shifting, as he gets farther into his 6th-grade year. During this specific lesson, she notices Kevin blurting out a combination of answers and off-topic remarks multiple times, distracting others from the lesson by making jokes, and ignoring the teacher's requests. At the end of the lesson, the bell rings and students get up out of their desks without permission. Kevin rushes out of the classroom and heads down the hall to math class. After class, Maggie approaches Ms. Smith to ask about getting samples of Kevin's work from last quarter. Ms. Smith hands Maggie a pile of student-made picture books and says that Kevin's story is in the pile—although when Maggie looks, she can't find it. Additionally, Kevin's folder of work, which is supposed to hold all of his work from the year, contains only four worksheets.

Kevin's 6th-grade year looked very different from his 5th-grade year. Although he was still a student at the same school, Kevin transitioned to the 6th- to 8th-grade building and into a middle school setting. He went from having Mr. Starks as his primary teacher to having four content teachers and three specialist teachers. During Kevin's 6th-grade year, there were multiple moments of disconnect between him and Ms. Smith, as well as changes in Kevin's behavior and attitude. As teachers, we make assumptions about students all the time. Ms. Smith, who was just meeting Kevin at that moment, made assumptions about who he was as a student that positioned him in deficit ways. When discussing Kevin during an informal interview with Lori, she called him "a behavior problem" and a student who "was immature and didn't care," rather than seeking to understand why Kevin was misbehaving in class and not turning in his schoolwork. A lack of initiative on her part positioned Kevin as an apathetic student, and marked a missed opportunity for her to give Kevin the "benefit of the doubt" and implement alternative practices steeped in trust and respect for Kevin.

We knew from Kevin's experiences in 5th grade that he was a student who cared about his learning. Teachers have the power to position students in both negative and positive lights, to privilege both personal and academic ways of knowing, and to help students negotiate their identities in school. Ms. Smith held an unfavorable story about who Kevin was in 6th grade—and ultimately this influenced Kevin's own stories of who he was as a person, student, reader, and writer.

As we dig more deeply into Ms. Smith and Kevin's relationship, keep in mind that classrooms are vibrant, complex, and often-chaotic spaces. The demands placed on the shoulders of teachers, coupled with the reality of fast-paced decisionmaking in the classroom, leave little time for reflection prior to action. For the most part, teachers are left on their own to negotiate classroom tensions, build respectful relationships with students, and cultivate learning environments that facilitate, rather than interfere with or shut down, robust learning. Below we explore the disconnect between Kevin and Ms. Smith, factors that played into their relationship, and possible paths that could have helped turn around the dynamics of their relationship and Kevin's engagement in language arts class.

A flurry of factors. An array of issues contributed to the disconnect between Kevin and Ms. Smith. Like many urban teachers today, Ms. Smith worked at a middle school with limited resources and within a larger education system that did not place value on cultivating meaningful relationships with students. School- and districtwide policies, school culture, and the level of resources available to teachers all play into the opportunities teachers have to build respectful relationships with students.

Like many teachers, Ms. Smith was juggling numerous academic objectives. She was a second-year, White, middle-class, monolingual teacher, working with predominantly linguistically diverse students from marginalized communities. As a new teacher, she was just beginning to build her toolbox of culturally sustaining resources. Ms. Smith did not have a structured curriculum that she followed. As a novice teacher, she had to spend a significant amount of time creating her language arts lessons, taking away time and energy that could have been spent getting to know her students and families in meaningful ways. Ms. Smith had 60 students and saw them in groups for 80 minutes each day, further reducing the number of opportunities she had during class time to get to know each person. This was Kevin's first year in a middle school environment, and this new system was an adjustment and hard for him at times.

After Maggie discovered that Kevin had very little work in his class folder, she and Lori set up a meeting with Ms. Smith to talk about Kevin's literacy accomplishments and engagement in class. Ms. Smith told them Kevin was failing language arts. They were shocked to hear this; Kevin had been one of the top three readers in Mr. Starks's class and had received "exceeds expectations" on the state reading assessment the previous spring. During this conversation, Ms. Smith talked about how she cared about Kevin, but she also expressed a deficit perspective about him. She described him as a student with "potential," but one who didn't care about or take responsibility for his own learning. She also spoke about the challenges of getting in contact with his mother because the teacher did not speak Spanish and Kevin's mother did not speak much English. In contrast, during the previous year Mr. Starks mentioned having frequent communication with Kevin's mother with the help of the school interpreter. Ms. Smith focused on Kevin's bad behavior and correlated this to him being a "class clown." Again, we noticed the contrast from the previous year, when Kevin's great sense of humor was used to engage him and others in meaningful reading lessons.

While Ms. Smith was in her second year of teaching, Mr. Starks was in his seventh year. It is probable that in addition to his focus on relationship building, Mr. Starks's years of experience played into his success as a teacher and into his ability to challenge his own thinking about who his students were and why his students were or were not engaged in literacy learning in school. Ms. Smith might have been able to help Kevin by pushing back on her own thinking about Kevin as a student who did not care about his learning.

Potential solutions. After Maggie had finished dialoging with Ms. Smith at school, she asked whether she could have some time to talk with Kevin. Maggie arranged a time to talk with Kevin and asked him what was going on in class from his perspective. Kevin broke down in tears and said that his mom and stepdad didn't know that he was failing language arts. Maggie and Kevin called his stepdad, who came down to the school immediately to talk with Maggie, Kevin, and the ELL teacher at Star Academy.

A critical move made in the instance above was to bring Kevin and his parents into the conversation about how best to support him to be successful in his language arts class. In this case, there was a happy ending—Kevin, his parents, Ms. Smith, and a team of educators were able to make a plan to get Kevin caught up with his schoolwork. The whole group put this plan into action and Kevin earned a B in language arts at the end of the year. However, teachers don't always have a team of people to help intervene and support students in the ways they need in order to be successful in school. Realistically, without a team of researchers who knew Kevin and his parents, our advice to a "future" Ms. Smith would be to work with the Spanish interpreter at the school, or another Spanish-speaking colleague, to provide frequent communication to students' families. Ms. Smith could call Kevin's home on a regular basis and share both positive and negative reports with his mother and stepfather. She also could arrange for another staff member whom Kevin had a trusting relationship with to check in with him about his schoolwork and meet with both of them. We know from Kevin's 5th-grade year that regular communication via the Spanish interpreter at Star Academy's elementary building was generative for Kevin's success at school and his relationship with Mr. Starks. Additionally, Ms. Smith could schedule visits to Kevin's and other students' homes during the school year.

Instructionally speaking, we would recommend that Ms. Smith make more attempts to bridge her students' lives to her language arts curriculum. For example, in 6th grade Kevin had aspirations to be an architect. Ms. Smith could use this information to plan a small digital research project, centered on future careers, that required students to create a multimodal presentation for the class. This digital inquiry into both informational and fictional texts could provide opportunities for students to engage in activities that mattered to them, practice the digital literacy skills expected of 6th-graders, and involve student voices in the learning/teaching process—an integral component of culturally sustaining practices.

Taking a step away from the particulars of this case, we want to share some common ways that teachers can give students the benefit of the doubt. A good place to start is to assume that students are kind and good, that they want to learn, and that they care about their learning. As researchers in this project, knowing the students and their families over the course of 6 years gave us a lot of insight into why students acted the way they did in school. What did that help us understand about Kevin's behaviors in 6th grade? Kevin loved to make people laugh. Multiple times during language arts lessons in 6th grade, we observed him blurting out a joke to his classmates. Ms. Smith read this behavior as "being disruptive." On the other hand, this instead could be read as Kevin using his strength of having a good sense of humor to make others laugh. Another example is Kevin's habit of continuing to work independently, ignoring Ms. Smith's requests for his attention. Instead of judging this action as intentionally not following directions, this could be read as evidence of Kevin's confidence and love for literacy—and his ability to be oblivious to others around him when he was engaged in something he liked to do. Getting to know students ultimately means caring about them. Then, if a student demonstrates a behavior that is disruptive, instead of automatically characterizing the student solely on that behavior, educators can assume that something else must be wrong because they know more than one story of who their students are and why they make the choices they do.

SUMMARIZING LEARNING

Throughout this chapter we described ways that teachers attempted to put getting to know their students at the forefront of their teaching. We considered the question, "How do you build relationships with students and their families when you don't speak their home language or come from the same cultural or discourse communities that they do?" We saw how Ms. Jacobson moved beyond a "just teach" teacher stance to provide academic support and care for Tong. We read about how Mr. Starks provided instrumental support for Kevin. Last, we considered how Ms. Smith could have engaged in a benefit-of-the-doubt treatment with Kevin and suggested ways for teachers to engage in recommended practices, such as working with school staff to ensure consistent and frequent communication with parents and using students' personal interests and digital tools to encourage engagement in the classroom.

Ultimately, educators need to acknowledge that systemic racial, linguistic, gender, and social class disparities exist, and then work to create links between students' home and school lives, while still meeting the expectations of the district and state curricular requirements. This is important but tricky work. Simply put, this means that teaching and learning begin with getting to know students, their families, their home communities, and the sociopolitical factors that influence their lives. Weaving this knowledge into instructional practices in the classroom and into the relationships built with students and their families is an integral step in the process of creating strong relationships with students. In the next chapter, we will explore the families' experiences with engagement practices used in the schools.

DISCUSSION QUESTIONS

- Reflect on the cultural/discourse communities you are a member of and how they may be similar to or different from those of the students you are working with.
- The emphasis of this chapter is on teacher and student relationships, specifically the dilemmas that arise when building relationships with students who come from different cultural and discourse communities. What is something you have learned about building relationships with students? Why is it important to do so? How are relationship building and literacy learning connected?
- Review the three *ways of knowing* strategies that were highlighted in this chapter. Have you used any of these strategies before? What ideas did you glean for trying out something new?
- How did Ms. Jacobson move beyond a "just teach" stance? Think about a time you have moved beyond a "just teach" stance in your own teaching or observed another teacher doing this. What strategies were used?
- Think about a time that you have leaped to conclusions about a student. What assumptions did you make about his or her behavior? Have you ever been on the receiving side of a teacher's negative assumptions?
- What is one thing from this chapter that you will take into your own teaching practice?

CHAPTER 5

School and Family Interactions

At a kitchen table in a comfortable apartment Ms. Cruz began to share her concerns about her son's school. She and Kevin arrived in the United States the summer before he started 1st grade. In our first interview, conducted in Spanish by Lori, Ms. Cruz expressed her worry about truly understanding how Kevin was doing at school because neither of them spoke English. During this conversation, Ms. Cruz described Kevin's previous schooling experiences in Mexico, where he had begun to learn to formally read in Spanish in kindergarten. She feared that the transition to learning English would be difficult, but believed that Kevin would learn quickly. Ms. Cruz, as well as Kevin's uncle and his grandmother, helped whenever they could. Kevin came home from school and taught his mother English words and pronunciations. At the beginning of 1st grade, Kevin's main homework was reading English language books that the teachers sent from school, but Kevin couldn't read them. Still, each night Ms. Cruz signed the reading log to indicate that he had done his homework because Kevin wouldn't go to school if the log had not been signed.

The second visit with Ms. Cruz happened at the same kitchen table. She spoke of Kevin's school progress and needs. Almost all of her responses about Kevin's progress began with, "the teacher says." While Kevin was learning quickly, Ms. Cruz shared her frustration about her own limited English skills. She stated [translated from Spanish], "I would really like to know English to help him better, because there are things he asks for my help in, and I try, but sometimes I can help him and sometimes there are things that I don't understand and I can't help him. So I'd need to learn to help him more." When Lori encouraged her to continue to support Kevin's language and literacies in Spanish, Ms. Cruz responded that, at conferences, Kevin's teacher discouraged her from helping her son learn Spanish at home. Although working in Spanish together had been a crucial way for her and Kevin to spend time together, she had come to feel that she shouldn't do that.

Ms. Cruz's worries and frustrations as a loving single mother with emerging English language skills reflect many of the issues that immigrant families have when sending their children to school in the United States. For educators, teaching children well involves understanding the potential barriers that families face. Yet, it is not only the barriers that teachers need to be aware of, but also the strengths that families bring as multilingual, transnational households with rich cultural traditions. In this chapter, we explore how educators can increase meaningful involvement with multilingual families. We analyze the connections and disconnections among the families, the school policies aimed at supporting family engagement, and students' schooling experiences in the classroom.

Throughout, we use the experiences of the families we met and the engagement practices used by the schools the students attended as jumping-off points. We share the knowledge that we gained from the families about how they supported their children on their academic journeys through school. We describe evidence and ideas about the families' sense of agency and access to resources during elementary school; the families' perceptions about their children's academic progress; and their aspirations for their children. Last, we offer strategies for increasing connections with families that can be implemented at the classroom and school levels.

FAMILY ENGAGEMENT

The term **family engagement** encompasses all aspects of connecting families with the schools and classrooms in which their children learn. In this section we examine how family engagement has expanded over the years to become an important part of schooling. We pay particular attention to 21st-century dilemmas and issues that come with expanded ideas of family engagement for both the families and the schools.

Redefining Family Engagement in School

Family and parental involvement has an impact on student achievement in school (Jeynes, 2010). As you saw in the vignette with Ms. Cruz at the beginning of this chapter, creating meaningful and sustained involvement across school and home contexts is a common challenge (Delgado Gaitan, 2012; Good, Masewicz, & Vogel, 2010). The increasing diversity of student populations in U.S. schools adds a layer of complexity to home–school communications. A diverse student population implies diversity of families, and this includes newly arrived immigrant families with home languages and cultural practices that differ from the White middle-class norms that schools were constructed upon (Tutwiler, 2005). In the opening vignette it

Essential Dilemma:
How can educational personnel create meaningful relationships with linguistically and culturally diverse families?

is clear that Ms. Cruz wants to support her son's learning but is stymied by the expectations of the teacher along with school practices that do not value her son's multilingual potential. It is clear that an expanded notion of family engagement is necessary to support multilingual and transnational families' engagement in their children's learning.

Conventional or traditional family engagement, according to Delgado Gaitan (2012), includes conferences, open houses, "meet the family" gatherings, and parent–teacher association (PTA) meetings. These types of activities are categorized as **unidirectional family engagement**. Unidirectional practices focus on what families can do to support school goals and the academic achievement of their children, not on what school communities and staff can do to work collaboratively with families.

Broader views of family engagement consider parenting, communicating, and supporting learning at home as part of family engagement. **Bidirectional family engagement** broadens the concept of working with families to include what school personnel can do to support families. In some cases schools offer parent centers run by bilingual parents who can connect families to resources both in and out of school (Ross, 2015). In essence, the school becomes the community center of the neighborhood, where adults and children are welcome. Another example of bidirectional family engagement is when schools offer classes in English or job skills for parents on site. This creates concrete instrumental support for improving the lives of families and therefore their children.

Barriers to Family Engagement

Many families, regardless of cultural, linguistic, or socioeconomic background, experience barriers to traditional modes of school involvement. Some examples of the barriers that we have heard from families and teachers include:

- Working full time or more
- Not having transportation to school
- Emerging language skills in English
- Reliance on their children to communicate school requirements and events
- Parents' difficulties with reading and writing in the home language
- Cultural differences between school expectations in their country of origin and the United States
- Prior uninviting or unpleasant experiences

Being a volunteer at school, attending conferences, or participating in PTA meetings is unlikely if not altogether impossible for some parents who experience barriers such as those listed above. It takes intentional and focused efforts on the part of the school to begin to address these roadblocks to community engagement.

FAMILIES' EXPERIENCES

The families we met with experienced primarily unidirectional engagement in their children's schools. Educational personnel held parent conferences, sent home information in the home languages of the families, and, in the later elementary years, began to use the Internet to set up "parent portals" in English to communicate with families. These one-way strategies reinforced the mindset that information coming from the school, and about the school, was more important than information coming from, or about, the home.

As noted in the list of barriers above, families in this project frequently experienced roadblocks to meaningful bidirectional home–school engagement. For example, despite Randolph Elementary having several Hmong interpreters at the school, some of the Hmong-speaking parents in our project felt uncomfortable calling the school—perhaps because of language barriers and unfamiliarity with school norms and policies. In our first interview with Chue's parents, there was a long interchange between the parents and the Hmong interpreter. We found out later that Chue's mother was telling the interpreter about how Chue was being bullied on the bus, and that this had happened more than once. The interpreter, who worked at the school, spent time explaining to the mother when to call the school and whom to ask for, assuring her that there were people she could speak with who could help. Yet it seems that she never felt comfortable enough to make that call. Over the years she reported that her only contact with the school occurred when one of her children was ill or when she attended parent–teacher conferences. Similarly, Tong's parents called the school when he was absent, but for all other issues they waited until conferences.

The majority of information exchanged between the families and their children's teachers occurred during parent–teacher conferences, frequently facilitated by interpreters. Chue's parents indicated that they changed schools to have access to the Hmong interpreter at the school. During 1st grade, Ms. Mohammed, Abdirahman's mother, told us that since there was no Somali interpreter at Randolph Elementary, she visited the school to watch him in class, but because of the language barrier, she did not talk with the teacher. By the time Abdirahman was in 2nd grade, Randolph Elementary had Somali-speaking interpreters working as teaching assistants.

Unidirectional parent engagement strategies such as sending notes in students' home languages, providing interpreters, and making school and classroom information available online, while keeping parents informed, are "insufficient in maximizing student achievement through parent involvement" (Delgado Gaitan, 2012, p. 307). As Ubah's father stated in an interview, "I would suggest, from the school, if there was a little more direction to what to do at home." He felt that the school was not communicating specific-enough suggestions to extend or support learning at home.

Family Practices to Support Schooling

Traditionally, educational personnel view family support for schooling in two broad ways: general parental practices and helping children with their school learning at home. General parental practices include providing food, shelter, and rest, and getting children to school on time. For many educators, the degree to which caregivers assist with the completion of homework often is viewed as the primary way of evaluating the level of involvement in a child's life. We found that the most common homework practices required of students involved reading for a set period of time each day at home, completing math practice worksheets, and/or completing writing or spelling assignments. During the first few elementary years, many teachers had parents sign off on a "reading log" or other type of statement attesting to the fact that their child completed his or her reading. As noted in the vignette with Ms. Cruz and Lori, there are limitations to using parents as witnesses to students' completion of their reading homework. Many parents we met with did not read in English and were left feeling uncertain about whether their child was reading or completing homework correctly. Nonetheless, they understood the ramifications of not signing the reading log for their child in school.

Based on our observations, the level of parental involvement with homework differed across the families. One mother went through her son's backpack every day after school. Another mother understood that her daughter would come home and unpack her backpack and tell her what homework needed to be done and what papers were to be signed and returned. Other parents structured routines that included homework before playtime, then dinner and bedtime.

Overall, the parents with whom we talked were intentional about helping their children complete work that the school assigned. Difficulties surfaced when the adults did not have the academic background or literacy skills to answer questions or evaluate whether their children were following directions appropriately. Even in those cases, however, parents often enforced routines so that their children could complete assignments independently, or they found other family members such as siblings or cousins who could help them more successfully.

Relationship with School Staff

Teachers know how important it is to keep parents informed about how their children are doing at school, yet the extent to which parents take academic information about their children to heart is dependent upon many factors, including the relationships they have with school staff (Yamamoto & Holloway, 2010). Transnational families in the United States encompass a broad range of economic backgrounds; however, the families with whom we engaged, and those of other students in the urban schools where we observed, were predominantly low income. All of the families had emerging English language skills, and in most cases these improved across the 6 years. If immigrant families are made to feel that their language and culture are seen as a detriment to academic achievement, as Kevin's mother was, they may not feel welcome at school (Arias & Morillo-Campbell, 2008).

The families in our project displayed great variation in their relationships with the schools and classrooms in which their children were placed. Many relied heavily on siblings' experiences and conferences to understand their children's academic progress. For example, Chue's family struggled with accessing teachers and academic opportunities such as summer school. His 6th-grade teacher mentioned that his parents attended Open House and conferences but they did not ask for any additional resources or support from the school, unlike some other Hmong families who asked for more books to read at home. What factors influence a family to ask for support from school? We wonder whether a parent first might need to feel that it is a school's responsibility to provide these resources, or to have some expectation that these materials are available. Stronger English language skills or a more extensive background in the U.S. school system also might make that request more likely. Regardless of the reason, because Chue's parents were not very assertive, the school personnel saw them as uninvolved in their son's education. Teachers didn't ask about their home life, home literacy practices, or any concerns they might have, and communication never improved over time. During parent–teacher conferences in the spring of 3rd grade, Chue's teacher indicated how important it would be for him to attend summer school in order to enhance his academic skills to prepare for the advanced content of the upper grades. Chue's parents indicated to his teacher that summer school was not an option because of the time and

> **Teaching Opportunity:** Use bilingual aides and community liaisons in a collaborative manner across grade levels. Meet with other teachers who have students with the same home languages to determine common needs for bilingual aides, thereby streamlining the time they spend talking to families.

distance to the summer school site; they did not live near the school and had no way of getting him there on a regular basis. The discussion ended there. There was no attempt to find an alternative solution, and Chue did not get the help he needed. This is a clear example of a situation in which tenuous connections between parents and educators have direct effects on students' learning.

Families Exercising Agency

In a spacious living room we sat with Ubah's mother when Ubah was in 1st grade. Ubah's father was out of the country on business, which was a frequent occurrence. Ubah and her brother were in constant motion within the house. Ms. Ahmed recently had given birth to Ubah's little sister and she was happy to talk about her eldest daughter. As we began to ask her questions in English, it was evident that Ubah's mother understood what we asked her. Repeatedly, she began to respond in Somali before the interpreter had a chance to translate the question. The interpreter would then translate Ms. Ahmed's response to us. Often, Ms. Ahmed would use English for short responses. She explained that she could understand most items that came home from school in English, such as newsletters and homework. In listening to Ms. Ahmed we learned that she saw her daughter as independent and an advocate for her own schooling experience. In particular, she mentioned that Ubah was very responsible about doing her homework and that if anything came home from school she would let her mother know about it right away. During this visit Ms. Ahmed shared that it was important to the family for Ubah to learn and know English well but it was just as important for her daughter to know her native language. Ms. Ahmed expressed, "We are Somali and it is important for Ubah to communicate with her grandparents who only speak the Somali language."

While the families we met faced many barriers to inclusion in the U.S. school system, they also overcame many and exercised agency and active support in their children's schooling, sometimes in ways that were not understood by teachers and school staff. For example, when Ubah's family was dissatisfied with her schooling experience, they abruptly removed her from Randolph Elementary and enrolled her in a local Afrocentric charter school with a large Somali population. This move was triggered by an event that was interpreted differently by Ubah's parents, her teacher, and the school staff. One day when Amy went to visit the 2nd-grade classroom to find Ubah, she wasn't there. In fact, Ubah had not been in class for a week due to a misunderstanding between Ubah's mother and the school. According to Ubah's teacher, Ms. Chan, Ubah's mother had talked with her at conferences about Ubah being tested for a designation as "gifted and talented," which would qualify Ubah for a magnet school that her brother attended. Ms. Chan told Ms. Ahmed that she didn't think that Ubah qualified for the gifted and talented program and shared some observational assessment data to support her opinion. Ubah's mother talked to the school principal, who concurred with the classroom teacher. Ubah had participated in a district-wide assessment and, based on those results, didn't qualify for gifted and talented services.

Soon after this conversation, Ms. Ahmed went to the magnet school to try to enroll her daughter, but Randolph Elementary personnel had already contacted the magnet school about the disagreement between Ms. Ahmed and Ms. Chan and about Ubah's results on the districtwide assessment. The teacher and principal from Randolph Elementary interpreted Ms. Ahmed's actions as her trying to "pull a fast one" and go outside of a system that had already told her no. Judging a parent's desire to change schools as subversive and questioning parents' beliefs that their child is gifted is a deficit perspective that did not serve to build a relationship, identify a solution, or support Ubah. This attitude boxed Ms. Ahmed into the passive role as "receiver" of the decisions made by school personnel. Through this experience, Ms. Ahmed was less likely to trust that the school staff had Ubah's best interests in mind. This event shut the door on an opportunity for Ms. Ahmed and Ms. Chan to discuss how Ubah's expertise and creativity could be brought forth within the classroom through an enriched curriculum. Further, it is illustrative of the ways in which school personnel failed to address the student's and family's needs and wants.

Ideally, school personnel would work with parents, who could contribute information about the child that would lead to academic success. Finding the right school for one's child is the ultimate act of parental involvement and agency within the school system. By exercising her parental decisionmaking in a way that looked different from what school officials expected, Ms. Ahmed challenged the assumptions some teachers hold about transnational families.

When Ubah was not allowed into the magnet school her mother enrolled her into a Somali Charter school, but Ubah only stayed at the school for a year. Dissatisfied with the instructional practices and curriculum at the charter school, Ms. Ahmed moved Ubah to a science/technology magnet school for her 5th-grade year. Between Ubah's 5th- and 6th-grade years, her family followed relatives and moved to a suburban area that they believed provided better educational opportunities for Ubah and her siblings. While Ubah was the only Somali girl in her grade at the suburban school, Ms. Ahmed and her husband asserted that the school provided a more challenging academic environment. During her 6th-grade year, Ubah's parents actively monitored her academic progress through an online student information system where they could check on grades and homework, and communicate with her teachers. Over the course of Ubah's elementary years, each move to a new school was designed to keep her on a stronger academic track.

In addition to Ubah, Kevin, the young Spanish speaker we learned about in the opening vignette, changed schools during his 3rd-grade year. Based on suggestions from a family member, Kevin's mother moved him to a charter school. She gave us three primary reasons for this change: First, the charter school had a Spanish-speaking parent liaison who was available and interested in speaking with parents about any issues they had questions about. Second, Kevin's mother wanted to get him away from a friend who his teacher said distracted him from paying attention in school. Third, the class sizes at the charter school were smaller.

As a research team, we wondered whether switching schools would be a disruption to Kevin's early success in acquiring the language and skills of school. However, this move ended up being positive and allowed Kevin's mother to become more engaged in school and Kevin to receive better instruction.

Understandings of Schooling

Tong's father, Mr. Vang, was very welcoming during our 1st-grade home visit. Sitting in their living room, Tong's parents shared that they immigrated to the United States from refugee camps in Thailand. Mr. Vang shared through the interpreter that he could read and write a little in Hmong. Tong's mother chimed in and told us that she was not able to read or write in Hmong very well. They both indicated that they were schooled in the Thai refugee camp and attempted to learn English but it was too hard to learn and balance family obligations. Tong spoke in both English and Hmong at home, but his parents said he preferred Hmong. Mr. Vang believed that Tong was learning faster than his 4th-grade sister, but most of their information was deduced from parent conferences. The parents asked us about home tutoring services for Tong's reading; they felt that they couldn't help him because they did not speak English and the teacher said that Tong needed to read more at home.

In 3rd grade we met with Tong's mother at their home again. We learned that the parents continued to believe that Tong was doing better than his sister but that he still struggled in reading. His mother said that she wanted him to read at school more because it was hard for her to know whether he was doing it right when he read at home. The parents relied on the three older siblings to help Tong, but they were often busy with their own work. She mentioned that Tong didn't talk about school with them. The parents had stopped asking questions about what happens at school because Tong often responded, "I don't know."

All of the families in this project indicated their desire for their children to learn English and do well in school, but their level of understanding of their children's academic progress varied greatly and often was based on their personal experiences of schooling in their home countries. The previous schooling experiences of families in their home countries varied widely. For instance, Abdirahman's mother was in high school in Somalia prior to the civil war that tore her country apart. After the civil war, her family became refugees in Kenya. She indicated that she wanted to send Abdirahman to preschool in Kenya but it was not affordable. Ubah's parents were both well educated. Ms. Ahmed, Ubah's mother, completed secondary school in Somalia, then for a short time attended a private tertiary school in Egypt. Ubah's father was a practicing physician in Somalia and Kenya before moving to the United States.

Another factor in understanding their children's schooling experience are parental beliefs about "the role of past academic performance in determining future performance, the reliability of feedback from the schools and issues of self-efficacy in supporting students" (Yamamoto & Holloway, 2010, p. 197). In other words, parents' and families' expectations for academic success depend on their beliefs in their children's ability, their understanding and trusting of teachers' reports of their children's academic achievement, and their own ability to support their children in their schoolwork.

All of the families we worked with believed their children were doing well, and many had aspirations for their children to excel further. In particular, they believed their children were learning enough English to obtain the **cultural capital** needed to be successful in academics and the larger society. Cultural capital includes sociocultural resources, such as language and education, that people draw upon to participate successfully within society. Certainly the students were learning more English as well as content-area academic skills. It is hard for parents to know whether the academic progress they see in their children represents good growth or not; and it certainly is hard for them to "read between the lines" of what they hear positive-intentioned teachers say at parent conferences. Some of the parents we interviewed could draw on their older children's experiences in school as they worked to support their younger children and assess whether the younger children's growth seemed adequate. Still, these comparisons were not always helpful. We found several cases in which parents were not fully cognizant of the difficulties their children were having with the academic curricula at school.

Tong's and Chue's parents indicated that effort was key to their children's success. Tong's parents reported that older siblings were too busy and Tong needed to work on his own. If he was confused about his homework, he should just do *something*. His father said, "If you don't know how to read, just copy the words down." However, both of Tong's parents expressed that they were unsure that their children were doing their homework correctly because of their own limited English. Chue's parents shared their belief that "if he keeps doing what he is doing now he will be better than his brother or sister." They were unsure of the scale for success at his grade level and had only general impressions about how he was progressing in comparison to his siblings. When they saw effort, they assumed this effort would be all that was needed.

A good starting place for teachers to support families is to obtain a clearer understanding of the parents' beliefs about effort and academic success. In Tong's case, his father believed that the important thing was that Tong was putting in effort on his homework. Yet, in both Tong's and Chue's cases, the boys struggled academically and whatever effort they put in was not quite enough to meet school expectations. Educators can create opportunities to engage families in conversations about the importance of effort and provide information and access to tangible resources that will build on students' personal effort to help them meet academic expectations.

WAYS TO ENGAGE FAMILIES

Sitting in a large living room around a low coffee table with a clear view of the kitchen table where Abdirahman was sitting, Lori and Carrie spoke with Ms. Mohammed for the first time. Ms. Mohammed told us that Abdirahman had never been to school before he entered kindergarten in the United States. Ms. Mohammed explained that she taught her children to read and write in Arabic through work with the Koran. She noted that the family spoke in Somali to one another and the children also spoke English among themselves.

A year later, Lori and Carrie sat around the same table and learned that Ms. Mohammed had found a larger home for her family and planned to move, but Abdirahman would remain at the same school. Ms. Mohammed saw a big change in her son in the year since 1st grade. He was now writing and reading in English, although she still worried about his vocabulary and how he always tried to complete his work very quickly. "When he slows down he does much better," she said. Ms. Mohammed had been going to school to learn English, and in subsequent family interviews she told us that a Somali interpreter would not be needed.

It was important to Ms. Mohammed that Abdirahman be bilingual. She shared with us that she often told him, "It is important to speak both languages." She continued, "I tell him, 'Do not forget both of your languages. English is all around the world. Somali is my special language and it is important.' Ms. Mohammed shared more details about the literacy practices that she and her children participated in at home, including going through a Somali/English dictionary and teaching her children vocabulary words in Somali and telling folklore stories from their culture. Ms. Mohammed concluded that she knew that reading and speaking with her son would help him be successful at school. She knew he was doing well at school because she contacted the teacher regularly.

Ms. Mohammed is an example of a parent who was eager to engage with the schooling processes of her children. Even though there was no Somali interpreter until late in Abdirahman's 1st-grade year, Ms. Mohammed would stop by to see her son in school and communicate with school personnel about his academic progress. Schools and classrooms encompass all sorts of families that want to be part of their children's experiences, but many traditional ways of thinking about family engagement fail to honor the multiplicity of ways in which families might participate.

In this section we share ideas for teachers and schools to help increase culturally relevant practices that can lead to authentic communication with families. At the school level, educational personnel can be encouraged to help parents learn about how U.S. schools function, what community services may be provided on site or nearby, and **two-generation approaches**—activities that involve families and children simultaneously. At the classroom level, individual teachers reflect on how to organize conferences for more meaningful interaction, including how to have thoughtful conversations with linguistically diverse families about their children's academic growth.

Key Components of Engagement

When working with linguistically diverse learners, culturally relevant engagement practices extend beyond the classroom and into the lived experiences of students and their families. Goodwin and King (2002) encourage teachers and school administrators to start from positive assumptions about families' engagement, in particular to believe that families want to be involved in their children's education. Another key assumption, or stance, that educators should keep in mind is that parents who are seen or present within the school do not represent the views and needs of all parents (Goodwin & King, 2002). In our interviews with families, we saw that parents want to both have a say and be informed about what is happening at school. Nonetheless, time, language differences, and a lack of reliable transportation to school events kept parents from becoming more involved.

Strategies for creating meaningful family engagement require three things from educators: (1) a commitment to working collaboratively toward a schoolwide mission of increased communication with families; (2) a mindset of openness and possibility to do this work despite, perhaps, previous failures; and (3) institutional support for meaningful communication between school personnel and families. An example that has all the components for meaningful family engagement is the Children's Literature Project in California, a project that brings together families to read and discuss the literature their children experience in schools. This program helped parents understand what the curriculum expectations were for their children while working on the parents' own English skills (Arias & Morillo-Campbell, 2008). This is also an example of a two-generation approach, involving both parents and children.

School Literacy

Programs like the Children's Literature Project, in which families are welcomed at school to discuss books with their children, are opportunities for families to learn about what is taught at school and understand how schools work (Delgado Gaitan, 2012). Much of what transnational parents know about how U.S. schools operate comes from their children's experiences with school or what they have heard from members of their cultural and linguistic community. The parents with whom we interacted had a variety of schooling experiences in their native countries, and they did not understand how grading works, how standards are set, what standards their children need to achieve, what tests are given and what those test scores mean, attendance procedures, or other district policies. Information of this type would have been helpful in print materials written in layperson's language in the families' home languages, in addition to during conversations with families at school events. While educational personnel share report cards with parents, these official documents often use terms for the skills that students are gaining that are unfamiliar outside of education (e.g., phonemic awareness or writing conventions). Report cards often are not very clear about the progress of students on a series of benchmarks across the elementary grades. Parents we spoke with commented that they often did not come away from parent conferences with sufficient information to know whether their child was meeting grade-level standards or not. As teachers share information about the expectations set for each grade level, it is also important that the conversation is two-way and that educators listen to what families have to say about their own expectations for the success of their children in the future.

Technology

Technology, including online parent portals, social media, texting, and automated voice messages, has been used in a variety of ways to facilitate communication with families and caregivers. In many school districts, automated messages to families are sent in each family's home language. There are also numerous web-based applications that can connect families to their children's classroom. While family engagement technology is a burgeoning field, there are still limitations to using technology. First, many technological approaches assume that families are literate in either their home language or English, and this is not always true. Another assumption is that families have access to and knowledge of how to use the technology needed to navigate the parent portals or websites. While using technology can be beneficial, it cannot be the only method of communication between schools and families.

Family–Child Conversations

One possibility for teachers to help improve parents' and caregivers' under-standing of the school experiences and accomplishments of their children is to help students communicate with parents and bridge the gap between school and home. In our interviews with parents, we found that very few of them learned much about what was going on at school from their chil-dren. Many of the children would respond in vague ways when asked what had happened at school. Some parents even mentioned that they had stopped asking their children about their school day. Communication between parents and children is essential not only to support language growth, but to bolster emotional well-being. Creating a daily classroom time to practice, in multiple languages, what happened at school will not only help the students internalize their learning for the day but help keep parents and children connected.

Daily conversations in the home between adults and children about school activities, such as science experiments, books, or special events, in-volve families in the school in what Jeynes (2010) has termed the "subtle aspects of parental involvement" (p. 753). Having students communicate about interesting books they read at school, or a new math game they learned, helps create an academically oriented home where families spend quality time talking about school and what is being learned rather than fo-cusing exclusively on the constraints of a homework assignment. Addition-ally, this provides a means for transnational families to gain cultural capital regarding the U.S. schooling system.

Examining Educator Assumptions and Expectations

A strategy that will go a long way toward helping teachers improve their relationships with families is for teachers to continually examine their per-sonal assumptions around parental and family engagement. Earlier in this chapter, we shared stories of families who changed their children's schools because they believed they would be better served in a new setting. When this happened, the students' current teachers wondered about the motivations of the families. As observers, and researchers and former teachers, we were concerned that changing schools, with differing procedures and support systems, would disrupt the emergent bilinguals' language acquisition and school success. We perceived the school that the students had started in as fully prepared to address the needs of emergent bilinguals. However, our long-term observations of the students, as they moved to different schools and systems, challenged our assumptions. Experiences with Kevin and Ubah taught us that the families worked hard to find a suitable caring academic space for their children.

Parent Conferences

Conferences or parent–teacher meetings are the most important way parents learn how their child is performing academically in school. Despite this, conferences are frequently rushed endeavors or disjointed because interpreters for families who don't speak English are often thinly spread throughout the school. Perhaps the simplest suggestion that we would offer teachers, based on our work, is to do more listening and less telling at conferences. In order to understand the parents' motivations, and not ascribe a lack of motivation to them, it is essential to hear their expectations for schooling and success. An emphasis on listening puts the onus on teachers to ask strategic questions. Providing time during your conferences to engage parents with questions such as, "What do you hope your child will learn this year?" and, "What are the types of activities you do with your child at home?" will help you access families' aspirations, needs, and potential barriers. The organization Colorín Colorado, whose aim is to improve the academic outcomes of multilingual students, offers a comprehensive website (www.colorincolorado.org/) with helpful ideas for teachers and principals to use to increase communication with multilingual students and families.

Honest and Supportive Conversations

Because learning a new language at the same time as learning academic content is a momentous task for students, there are likely to be tough conversations with parents about how students are or are not meeting standards. Over and over, the parents with whom we interacted told us that they believed their children were doing well based on information that they received from teachers. While many of the students in fact were doing well, others, like Chue, struggled to gain English proficiency throughout their elementary years. Parents need an accurate assessment of their child's academic progress so that they can encourage and reinforce academic goals (Yamamoto & Holloway, 2010).

Family engagement is crucial to student success, but knowing what is most beneficial for linguistically diverse families requires thoughtful reflection. In this chapter you have read about how family expectations differed based on a variety of factors such as parents' level of education, siblings' success in school, and families' cultural values. Each of the families we met with annually declared the importance of their children maintaining their home language in addition to learning English. Other families wanted their children to become leaders within their cultural communities, and they knew that this goal required the students to be bilingual. Still, most of the students we observed entered middle school below the proficiency levels set by the school district for mastering English. The desires of parents and children to be academically successful did not match how success was defined by educators and academic standards. This mismatch requires teachers to engage in honest conversations with families about what the academic demands of the school district are, without losing sight of the whole child, the dispositions the child has toward learning, and other capabilities. In other words, conversations between educators and families need to be about each individual emergent bilingual student's needs and abilities in relation to the standards set by the school or state.

Given this backdrop, how can teachers have conversations with parents about students' English language and academic development without creating disappointment and negative feelings on the part of the families and students? This is hard. As you have learned in this book, the rate at which emergent bilinguals acquire English language skills varies. Language benchmarks that the state or school has set are important, but may seem too stringent or unattainable to some educators. It is crucial for educators to help parents understand this dilemma and still maintain positive expectations for their children. First, educational personnel must see multilingual families who are learning English themselves as a resource for their children's success. Second, validating the capacity of students and families to become fully multilingual, and noting progress along that trajectory, can make parent conferences much more asset-based events. For this to happen, it is essential that educators cultivate real relationships with families. Creating meaningful bidirectional relationships with families takes effort by both individual teachers and school-level administrators, and often involves intermediaries such as bilingual school liaisons. As we have outlined, these relationships will require ongoing commitment and perseverance.

CONCLUSION

The families with whom we interacted engaged differently with schools. A few families demonstrated direct engagement with their child's school experience by showing up at school or moving their children to other schools where they felt more support. Some families supported their children's school experiences by creating routines and attending conferences. The parents' own level of literacy and English proficiency factored into the types of support they were able to provide. As described earlier, cultural models of parenting, families' socioeconomic background, advice from teachers, and other factors influence parents' beliefs about what they can do to support their children at home and school (Yamamoto & Holloway, 2010). While the families we visited represented great variation in their levels of literacy in the home language and English, one thing remained constant across the years and interviews: Parents wanted their children to be multilingual. See Sing's family felt that multilingualism was important so that she could help her community. Her father continued to teach her to read and speak Hmong as they both learned English. Ubah's family wanted her to be able to independently navigate the English- and Somali-speaking worlds through her bilingualism. Being bilingual also connected these students to their grandparents and extended families. Making connections to home language and culture in the classroom is only one step in ensuring that students feel welcome and cared for in the classroom. In order to reinforce emergent bilingual students' academic success, critical conversations about language development and academic support need to take place between teachers and families.

SUMMARIZING LEARNING

The essential dilemma that we explored in this chapter is how educators can increase meaningful involvement with transitional and multilingual families. Skills for working with and understanding multilingual and transnational families are essential for teachers to better structure appropriate learning environments. Working with families will look different depending on school location and populations; however, there are research-based ideas that apply across a number of contexts. School culture and individual teacher beliefs about working with families have a great impact on what actually happens in schools. Conversely, the beliefs that families hold about school also contribute to their participation in school events and processes. We described the gap that often exists between the family's perceptions of achievement, or school success, and how the children actually are performing in relation to academic expectations. These differences in perception can negatively impact student achievement over the long term if they mask the need for additional resources. Educators should create relationships that honor the aspirations of families and provide ways to support families in meeting their expectations of success.

QUESTIONS FOR REFLECTION AND DISCUSSION

- What are traditional and nontraditional ways for schools to engage with families? Why is it important for educational personnel to develop multiple ways to engage families?
- How do the ideas of unidirectional and bidirectional family engagement apply to how your school practices family engagement? Are there current practices that fit in both categories? Are there areas for improvement at your school?
- Reflect on your own family's involvement during your elementary years. How were your parents involved in your schooling? Were there aspects of your family's situation that made it easier to access schools and relate to teachers?
- Which part of the chapter resonated with you the most? Why?

CHAPTER 6

A Wide-Angle Lens on Curriculum

In this chapter we delve into a comprehensive topic: What was the elementary school experience like for the students we followed from 1st grade until their graduation from 6th grade? We examine the settings and curricula that students received through the elementary grades and analyze how these impacted their experiences. Because we know that educators are looking for models to help them address all of their learners within the classroom and schoolwide, we offer illustrative examples of programs for emergent bilinguals that provide frameworks and effective approaches that may be put into practice in a variety of settings. Following the students across multiple grades gave us a unique opportunity to see, through students' experiences, the content of schooling. From this wide-ranging perspective, we use this chapter to inquire into how the quality and consistency of programs and curricula affected students' language and content learning. How did each year's content build off the previous year's? Was the curriculum coherent, coordinated, and well-articulated to students and families? The dilemma we tackle in this chapter relates to the ways that the year-by-year cycle of schools may lead to disjointed experiences for students. Emergent bilinguals, especially those who are new to the United States, are at risk of receiving watered-down, isolated instructional experiences that may lead to a greater gap between them and their native English-speaking peers. The students we highlight have a tremendous need for relevant instruction based on meaningful assessments.

The six students you've read about started together in 1st grade at a public school, Randolph Elementary. At the beginning, they were all part of a program (described in the next section) that was specially designed for students who were not yet proficient English speakers. In 3rd grade, the students transitioned to mainstream classrooms within the same school and received ELL services in collaboratively co-taught classrooms (also described below). After 3rd grade, however, the students' school settings and service models began to vary. While three students, Chue, See Sing, and Tong, stayed at Randolph throughout, Abdirahman, Kevin, and Ubah changed schools. Abdirahman's and Kevin's families moved them to charter schools, where they received no ELL support, for 4th through 6th grades. Abdirahman's family was attracted to a charter school because of the focus on African culture and a large number of Somali-speaking staff. Kevin's mother decided that he should go to a nearby school that members of her community recommended because she felt that his poor behavior was becoming an issue at Randolph. Ubah's family tried two different schools—a charter school and a different public school—before settling at a suburban middle school when she was in 6th grade. Table 6.1 outlines the school settings and ELL services the students received throughout the elementary years.

In this chapter we examine the students' experiences in different "eras" of their elementary years: primary (1–2), middle (3–4), and upper elementary grades (5–6). Next, we dig into the concerning finding that the lack of continuity across their 6 years of elementary schooling may have led to students falling through the cracks. Finally, we offer some suggestions for educators to help design and implement a coordinated and cohesive program that supports emergent bilingual students' development over time.

PRIMARY GRADES: STARTING OUT IN SCHOOL

On the first day of 1st grade, the six children in this book came to Randolph Elementary from very different backgrounds. Some had been to Head Start and kindergarten. Some had been to school in another country. And some of the students had never set foot in a school before. Although their preschooling experiences were different, they all came together in their 1st-grade classroom because of their need for instruction that took into account their level of understanding and production of oral English. At some point, either in their last days of kindergarten or as they registered at the district office, the students had been given an assessment of their English language proficiency. They likely sat across the table from an adult who asked them to identify the English words for objects in pictures

Table 6.1. School Settings and ELL Service Type

	1st	2nd	3rd	4th	5th	6th
Abdirahman	LA PS	LA PS	ELL PS	MS CS	MS CS	MS CS
Kevin	LA PS	LA PS	ELL PS	MS CS	MS CS	MS CS
Chue	LA PS	LA PS	ELL PS	ELL PS	ELL PS	ELL PS
See Sing	LA PS	*ELL PS	ELL PS	ELL PS	ELL PS	ELL PS
Ubah	LA PS	*ELL PS	ELL PS	MS CS	MS PS	MS SPS
Tong	LA PS	LA PS	ELL PS	ELL PS	ELL PS	ELL PS

LA = Language Academy; ELL = English language learner services; MS = mainstream (no ELL support); PS = public school; SPS = suburban public school; CS = charter school
*Transitioned midyear

shown to them and to retell a story after they listened to a recording of it. The six students we followed all scored in the lowest level on their English language assessment—speaking English minimally in short words and phrases. This assessment of their English proficiency, in addition to the answers their caregiver gave on a home language questionnaire, made them eligible for a special district program for students who needed extra support in English.

As discussed in Chapter 2, many schools and districts have a special plan in place for newcomer students who have the least English proficiency and/or are new immigrants to the United States. This program, Language Academy, provided up to 2 years of intensive language support for these students, many of whom may have had limited or interrupted formal education. To qualify for Language Academy initially, students must have had fewer than 2 years of formal education in the United States and/or very low English-proficiency levels. The program was designed to provide students with English language development, grade-level content, and an opportunity to participate fully in the school and larger community. For part of the day, students participated in mainstream classes in which they engaged in grade-appropriate curriculum. For the other part, they received intensive English language instruction in a separate classroom with other newcomer students. General education teachers and ELL specialists provided instruction collaboratively throughout the day—sometimes working together in the grade-level classroom and sometimes in separate spaces.

A Look into a Primary-Grade Newcomer Class

In 1st and 2nd grades, the six students spent most of their day in their mainstream classrooms, but for 90 minutes in the mornings they came together for a Language Academy literacy block that intertwined reading, writing, and language instruction. The 1st- and 2nd-grade ELL teachers, Ms. Lansing and Ms. Green, pooled their resources and their students into one classroom. Doing this allowed them to co-teach and differentiate instruction through grouping, which they couldn't do as effectively on their own. A typical day of their literacy block included whole-group interactive language activities, a differentiated reading workshop, and word study. Table 6.2 shows typical activities during the block.

Ms. Lansing and Ms. Green immersed students in language and literacy instruction throughout the block because they felt it was essential that students develop oral language and literacy skills concurrently. Teaching language didn't mean only explicit vocabulary or grammar instruction—singing, chanting, and playing games served as vehicles for learning the rhythm of language, providing language practice, and scaffolding students' use of language. Notice how Ms. Green infuses language instruction into her literacy block in the following lesson.

Table 6.2. Language Academy Literacy Block

Interactive language	Whole group	• Thematic • Chants, poems, songs • Interactive read-aloud • Shared reading • Vocabulary building • Discussion and verbal interaction • Follow-up writing extensions
Reading workshop	Small group/ independent	• Guided reading • Authentic literacy activities (familiar reads, literacy games, books on tape) • Independent reading and reading response • Oral language groups using photo cards, led by volunteers or aides
Word study	Whole group/ small group	• Shared reading of phonics readers • Spelling feature sorts • Differentiated phonics instruction based on developmental stage

As a new learning period starts, Ms. Green calls 20 students to their carpet spots and pushes play on the CD player. The students jump up before the song starts—it's one they sing often in class and they know just what to do.

"Red!" (Ms. Green holds up a red flashcard with the word "red" written on it.)

"I see something red." (She holds her hand above her eyes as if searching for something.)

"Red, red, red, red. I see something red. Find something red!" (Students all look around the room for red items.)

Although not all of the students are singing aloud, they are paying close attention so that they can find a red classroom item. On cue, they begin to point to objects around the room and say their names: "Marker! Apple!" After a couple of rounds of the song with different colors, the students sit on the carpet, still talking about the colors in their sweatshirts and on their shoes. The next song starts and children chime in using hand motions to match the words.

"Hello, hello, hello how are you?"

"I'm fine, I'm fine, I hope that you are too."

Ms. Green calls individual students' names to stand and sing the different parts of the song to one another. Some students participate with gusto, while the quavering voices of others can barely be heard. Still, all are part of the community and welcome their friends to school.

In this activity, the students have the opportunity to use new English words and phrases over and over again in a fun and engaging way. They are able to understand the language being used (receptive language) and eventually use it themselves (productive language). In Ms. Green's lesson, it is not likely that any of the students would have been able to express a sentence like, "I'm fine, I hope that you are too," on their own, but in their daily song they are able to produce the phrase with support and interact in a fun way.

Midyear in 2nd grade, Ms. Green and the general education teachers decided that See Sing and Ubah should be transitioned from the Language Academy literacy block to their mainstream classrooms. These students were making good progress in reading and writing and they participated verbally in class. They were easily incorporated into their mainstream classrooms for readers' and writers' workshop and continued to get ELL services for about an hour a day during math time. The other four students continued in the specially designed Language Academy class for the full 2 years allotted to them by the district.

At the end of their second year in Language Academy, Ms. Green reflected on the growth of some of the students. Abdirahman, she said, was at the top and doing "fabulously." He was a leader in the large group, constantly raising his hand to participate. She described his English as "close to fluent." According to Ms. Green, Abdirahman was ready to be fully mainstreamed. As for Kevin and Chue, Ms. Green was less certain about their readiness. She noted that Kevin had spent his first year in Language Academy "pretty much out of it"; but he must have been listening, because this year she saw his hand shooting up and showing her his "knowledge of social and academic language." Kevin's reading also was really progressing. Chue, however, was more of a "struggler." According to Ms. Green, he was very slow at picking up the language and reading parts of the curriculum. "We'll pull him along," she said, "but we've got a lot to work on."

MIDDLE ELEMENTARY: HITTING THE MAINSTREAM

By 3rd grade all six students were in mainstream educational programs. Instead of spending much of their day with new emergent bilinguals and an ELL specialist to teach them, the students were now fully integrated into mainstream classes. The mainstream classes were made up of native English-speaking students as well as emergent bilinguals with a variety of proficiency levels. The six students we observed were now spread across four different 3rd-grade classrooms. Socially and academically, they were in new territory.

The mainstream curriculum posed quite a challenge for these students. Although all of the teachers at Randolph Elementary used the districtwide framework of balanced literacy instruction through readers' and writers' workshops, the instruction was not nearly as explicit, interactive, or scaffolded as in the earlier grades or specially designed ELL classes. Reading and writing expectations were more demanding, and students were expected to do much more independent work than in earlier grades. Students participated in differentiated small groups but also experienced more "sit and get" time than before. Songs, skits, and games were rare, replaced by chapter book read-alouds, whole-class discussions, and individual written responses. Overall, in 3rd and 4th grades the expectations were ramped up and the supports were reduced. And while some of the students had the skills and dispositions to face the challenge, others were less prepared.

Fortunately, as the focus students entered the turbulent waters of the mainstream, they were not without a flotation device. In many schools, students are left to "sink or swim" on their own after exiting newcomer programs. For some students, this sudden inattention can cause academic English and content-area learning to slow as they struggle alone to get their bearings. Here, services for English learners were coordinated across a continuum based on the English-proficiency level of the students. Students who had the least English and the greatest need for support were enrolled in Language Academy. As students gained proficiency over the years and became more able to participate in the mainstream classroom, the support was pulled away gradually (see Figure 6.1). Across the continuum, students and families also benefited from the help of bilingual educational assistants who provided written translations of school documents, classroom interpretation when needed, and language-specific family meetings.

Figure 6.1. Articulation of ELL Support Across the Elementary Years

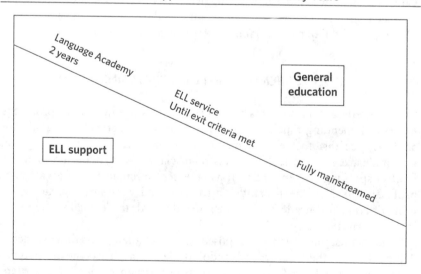

Serving English Learners in the Mainstream

At Randolph Elementary, teachers used a **collaborative instruction** approach to serve their emergent bilingual students. Collaborative instruction takes place when at least two teachers with different areas of expertise work together, often in one classroom, to meet the needs of the students. Although educators collaborate in many ways in schools, such as planning for fieldtrips or sharing bus duty, collaborative instruction for emergent bilinguals is focused on teaching (Dove & Honigsfeld, 2010). By working together throughout the teaching/assessment cycle, co-teachers put their heads together to make the best instructional decisions for all students. Plus, having two adults in the classroom together means that instructional duties can be shared and the teacher–student ratio is reduced.

There are many potential benefits to this approach for instructing emergent bilinguals. Instead of being pulled out of the classroom for ELL class, students stay with their classmates and get access to the regular grade-level curriculum. Yet, they continue to receive much-needed support and language instruction through access to a co-teacher who works with them individually and in small groups, or even teaches the whole class. Emergent bilinguals in co-taught classrooms feel more included and develop more varied relationships, including friendships with non-ELL students. Academically, collaboratively co-taught classrooms provide an environment in which students participate more, behave better, and are more challenged (York-Barr, Ghere, & Sommerness, 2007). Not only is there a benefit to the students, but collaborative teachers report that working side-by-side and sharing the same students and instructional space increases their own professional learning (Frederick, 2013). Below, we take a closer look at the ways that this collaborative approach supported the focus students at Randolph Elementary.

A Look into a Collaboratively Co-Taught Classroom

At Randolph Elementary, the six focus students were in regular 3rd-grade classrooms and received between 30 minutes and 1½ hours of ELL services through collaborative instruction, depending on their language and literacy needs. Typically, co-teaching occurred during part of the 2½-hour literacy block, which consisted of readers' and writers' workshop as well as word work activities. The ELL teachers came to the grade-level classrooms at the beginning of the workshop period and stayed throughout the lesson, after which time they would move on to a different classroom. While in the room, the ELL teacher participated meaningfully in the lesson and became an equal part of the teaching partnership. When schools employ a pull-out model of ELL service, it is common for an ELL teacher to work with many small groups of students from a large number of classrooms and often for shorter time periods.

Amy observed the following lesson in the 3rd-grade classroom of See Sing, Tong, and Kevin. In this lesson on how to do a book talk with their 6th-grade reading buddies, you can see how the two teachers worked with students in a variety of ways to support specific student needs. Ms. Vu is the 3rd-grade teacher, and Ms. Jones is the ELL teacher.

Twenty-three students are sitting cross-legged on the carpet, and two teachers are sitting at the front of the group, one near an easel with chart paper. Ms. Vu begins by telling the 3rd-graders that their 6th-grade reading buddies will be visiting tomorrow and that they will be expected to do a book talk with their buddy. As Ms. Vu is speaking, Ms. Jones writes "Book Talk" at the top of the chart paper. Ms. Vu asks the students to turn and talk to a partner about what they think makes a good book talk. As students turn to each other, both teachers move down to the carpet to facilitate the conversations of partners who need support, especially emergent bilinguals. After a minute, the students turn back to the front and raise their hands to offer suggestions to the teachers while Ms. Jones scribes their contributions on the chart. Ms. Jones now grabs a favorite picture book and models a quick book talk using straightforward language and pointing to each part of the talk as she completes it. Ms. Vu asks if there are questions and sends the students off with partners to practice book talks and then continue reading from their book bags. She rings a bell and the students are off to gather their books and sit at tables and floor spots around the room.

While it's true that this mini-lesson could have been conducted by just one teacher, having two allowed them to provide extra scaffolds for student understanding and participation. For example, while Ms. Vu was providing an overview of book talks verbally, Ms. Jones was simultaneously providing a visual cue of the same information on a chart that students could refer to throughout the lesson. Also, when students were sharing ideas with their partners, two teachers were able to listen in and provide guidance, which means that twice as many students received this support. As the students moved on to work time, the teachers divided their roles intentionally in order to support independent practice and provide instruction to small groups of students.

Ms. Jones sits at a kidney-shaped table and pulls out a tub with her teaching resources. She calls five emergent bilingual students to the table to work with her. For 20 minutes, the students read and discuss a leveled text, which they put in their book bags. Before sending them to work independently, Ms. Jones asks each student which book they are going to use for the book talk and reminds them of the expectations. Concurrently, Ms. Vu is circulating among the student partners to keep students on track and help as needed with their practice book talks. She now moves to a different table and calls six students to work with her in a guided-reading group, while Ms. Jones works with another, more advanced group of emergent bilingual students and the remaining students read independently.

After the 40-minute work period, Ms. Vu gathers students on the carpet again for sharing time. Ms. Vu has asked two students to present their book talks in front of the class. After the students share, their classmates say what they noticed about their book talks and give compliments. See Sing raises her hand and says, with a little support from Ms. Jones, that she liked the way the student started her book talk with a question.

In this lesson, both teachers had important instructional roles to play. Ms. Vu conducted the initial whole-group lesson, supported partner practice, facilitated a guided-reading group, and led the final share time. Ms. Jones scribed the chart, modeled a book talk, completed two small-group language development sessions, and encouraged the participation of emergent bilingual students in the whole group. Having two expert teachers and a well-planned lesson clearly benefited the students in this class.

The students we observed all entered 3rd-grade classrooms in which they were served by the collaborative model. Based on their academic and linguistic needs, they experienced whole-group, small-group, and sometimes one-on-one instruction from the ELL teacher. This support helped to ease their transition from their newcomer classroom, but may not have been enough to ensure their achievement with grade-level literacy skills and performances.

UPPER ELEMENTARY: A TORRENT OF CONTENT

As the students we worked with entered 5th and 6th grades, their challenges increased. In these grades, the focus on academic content areas—such as history, algebra, and biology—increased, and students were expected to become independent, strategic learners as they prepared for secondary school. Intermediate students were asked to comprehend complex texts, use academic vocabulary, write and speak persuasively, and use language to convey higher order thinking in all content areas. Emergent bilinguals are at risk of falling behind during these pivotal grades, and schools often struggle to implement best practices for them. Nationwide, intermediate-grade English learners perform poorly on standardized assessments such as the National Assessment of Educational Progress (NAEP) test. In 2013, for example, 93% of 4th-grade students identified as English language learners scored below the proficient level in reading (Kids Count Data Center, 2013).

Although the upper elementary grades are a potentially risky period for multilingual students, this is also the time when students may no longer receive ELL services. Students who were born in the United States or came with their parents when they were small children often enter the U.S. education system when they are 4 or 5 years old. Civil rights laws upheld by the U.S. Department of Education and the U.S. Department of Justice mandate that schools offer ELL services until students are proficient in English and can participate meaningfully in educational programs without linguistic support. Nonetheless, cash-strapped schools and districts are left on their own to determine what "proficiency" and "meaningful participation" look like. Because of this, students may be exited from ELL services before they are ready. Alternatively, some students never achieve the proficiency needed to exit ELL services and find themselves "stuck" in ELL classes in secondary schools even though they've been in the United States for many years. These students are commonly called **long-term English learners** (Menken, Kleyn, & Chae, 2012). Exiting emergent bilinguals either too early or too late raises civil rights concerns. Students who are exited too soon may be denied access to supportive ELL services, while students who are exited too late can be denied access to segments of the general curriculum necessary for academic growth; this, in turn, contributes to a higher risk of dropping out of school (U.S. Department of Education, Office of English Language Acquisition, 2015).

Of the six students we highlight in this book, three had been transitioned to receiving no ELL services by 4th grade and three continued to receive some support. By the end of their elementary years, Chue, See Sing, and Tong fit profiles common to many long-term English learners. Often these students have mastered basic reading skills such as phonics and word recognition, yet struggle to read, write, and comprehend the academic English used in the classroom. Studies confirm that many adolescent children from linguistically diverse families have very low vocabulary levels, which, in turn, affects their literacy and general academic success (Lesaux & Marietta, 2012).

In 5th and 6th grades, Chue, Tong, and, to a lesser degree, See Sing, were struggling in academic areas. Their teachers did what they could to meet the needs of these students by building in developmental English language and literacy instruction and scaffolding academic content work, but at this point it felt like the students were so far behind the grade-level standards that teachers questioned whether they would be able to catch up. During literacy instruction teachers used differentiated grouping to work with students at their instructional reading levels. In one classroom Ms. Petersen, a 6th-grade teacher, and Mr. Parks, an ELL teacher, collaborated during readers' workshop so that they were able to meet with their lowest reading groups nearly every day. Chue, Tong, and See Sing were among them. While in those groups, students read and discussed leveled texts from their reading curriculum and focused on using reading strategies to comprehend text. Mr. Parks explained, "While we are introducing the strategies they need to use, I am often introducing the language in order for them to engage academically with the topic."

Mr. Parks also worked with the students regularly in a small English language development (ELD) group. ELD instruction is designed specifically to advance emergent bilinguals' knowledge and use of English in increasingly sophisticated ways. The ELD curriculum emphasizes the development of all four language domains: reading, writing, listening, and speaking, and is differentiated in order to meet the needs of students who are at various levels of English language development (Saunders, Goldenberg, & Marcelletti, 2013).

Even though Chue, See Sing, and Tong participated in specially designed reading groups and received ELD instruction, their progress was slow. Their teachers observed that they lacked confidence and were timid about participating in their 6th-grade classrooms. Their academic skills lagged behind the native English-speaking students in class and the gap continued to widen. These teachers provided all of the support they could muster using best practices and high-quality curricular materials to guide their approaches. Yet, this widening gap posed a significant concern for the teachers. What else could they do to accelerate student learning?

Essential Dilemma:
How can teachers provide a cohesive curriculum for emergent bilingual students when they work with them for only 1 year?

This concern leads to the central dilemma of this chapter. Certainly, all educators hope that their students will achieve academically. Yet we know that some will be less successful than others based on a number of factors. Why is it that some students "take off" and others don't? Teachers want to know more about how to design curriculum to keep emergent bilinguals moving forward and ensure their continued growth in language and literacy. While teachers may have an understanding that language learning takes time and patience, there is also a sense of urgency to accelerate their progress and close the language and literacy gap between emergent bilingual students and their native English-speaking peers. How can educators provide a cohesive literacy and language curriculum that nudges students toward the high standards we have for all students? In the next section, we look back over the 6 years of this project for insights on how this tension played out for the six focal students and their teachers.

A CONCERNING FINDING

One of the advantages of longitudinal projects like this one is that we have the opportunity to see a set of student experiences as a whole in a way that teachers are not usually privy to. The typical rhythm of school is marked by 9-month segments in which teachers and students have intense relationships that end with a wave of the hand as the last school bus pulls out and summer vacation begins. As we look back from our unique vantage point across the 6 elementary years of the focal students, we see repetitive patterns, rare moments, and missed opportunities that are obscured in the predictable momentum of the school year.

The six students featured in this book had quality educational experiences. They were in reputable elementary schools, had access to a number of resources, and were taught by competent educators using best practices. And yet, not all of them were equally ready for the leap to secondary school at the end of their elementary years. When we ask ourselves why this is the case, the answer is elusive. As we learned in Chapter 2, there are many factors involved in language and literacy development, and pinpointing which of these factors might be the root cause of a later challenge is not possible. Nonetheless, one of the recurring key issues that arose over the years concerns the curricular program experienced by the students. Three of the students (Chue, See Sing, and Tong) stayed at the same school throughout their elementary years, and three students (Abdirahman, Kevin, and Ubah) moved to one or more additional schools. The students who left the public school district to attend a new public or charter school received a very different curricular program. Each move required an adjustment period for the students and their families as they got used to new pedagogical approaches, classroom environments, behavioral expectations, and family engagement activities. Ubah, for example, attended four different schools in 6 years and moved from a curriculum based on the workshop model, to one with a cultural focus, to a museum-based magnet, to a traditional, teacher-centered approach. Ubah and her family adapted well, but along the way her "school history" was lost. Each move was like starting over in the collective knowledge at the site. None of the teachers knew what had happened at the previous school so there was a profound discontinuity in the instruction she received. Although troubling, this is hardly surprising considering the ways that the education system works. Changing schools often leads to disjointed and uncoordinated experiences. From this perspective, the students who stayed in the same school should reveal the opposite—a well-coordinated journey that builds from one year to the next and provides continuity and stability.

And yet, of the six students we report on in this book, the three who stayed at the same school throughout—Chue, See Sing, and Tong—could be described as the least academically successful at the end of elementary school. On assessments given in their 6th-grade year, they were below grade level in all content areas, and their English language levels were intermediate at best (see Table 6.3). This is troubling because one would hope that after 6 years of quality education in the United States (more, for those who attended Head Start and kindergarten), the students would be performing similarly to their non-ELL peers. Research indicates that students who arrived before the age of 8 with little or no formal schooling typically take 7–10 years to reach grade-level norms in English language literacy (Hakuta, Butler, & Witt, 2000).

Looking back at the educational stories of See Sing, Chue, and Tong, we did see some commonalities. For example, in interviews with their grade-level teachers, we often heard what good children they were. Teachers described them as "well behaved," "trying hard," and "working to the best of their abilities." Chue's 3rd-grade teacher shared:

> Chue works hard. I think he will be okay going into 4th grade. He is not the only kid at a 2nd-grade (reading) level. He's not afraid to ask questions when he's stuck. He knows he's below grade level but it doesn't stop him. There are no confidence issues.

Of course, being hard-working is a tremendous asset to the students overall, but the teachers' focus on student effort and classroom behavior seemed to mask the underlying concern about their lack of language and literacy skills.

After 3rd grade, these three students were no longer the least proficient English speakers in their classes. Other newcomers were arriving every year

Table 6.3. Sixth-Grade Assessment Data

	Reading grade level	Spelling stage	English language level (1–5)	MAP reading score (mean = 212)
Abdirahman	7	Derivational relations	5	220
Kevin	6	Late within word pattern	5	213
Ubah	6	Syllables and affixes	5	219
See Sing	4	Late within word pattern	4	189
Chue	3.5	Early within word pattern	3	186
Tong	3.5	Early within word pattern	3	177

with lower English proficiency and greater language and literacy needs. So, while the students we describe were performing below grade-level expectations, there was not a sense of concern or urgency about their progress among their teachers. Rather, teachers expressed a caring understanding that language learning takes time and that students with lower levels of English language were not able to perform well on standardized measures. For example, Chue's 3rd-grade ELL teacher generously predicted, "He is going to get it. It's going to click and he will make more rapid progress." Teachers did not fret if students' writing was difficult to understand because of the many spelling and grammatical errors. Nor were teachers anxious about students' reading comprehension because the texts, although at their instructional level, often were about topics in which the children had little background knowledge, or contained rare vocabulary or complex structures. It's not that the teachers didn't notice these things—they did. They used adequate diagnostic assessments and developmental rubrics, and took some observational notes. They could describe the specific struggles of the students. It's more that the teachers knew that the students weren't performing well and excused it as long as the students were putting forth good effort. More often than not, the three students who stayed at Randolph were flying under the radar. And the problem, of course, with flying under the radar is that they received little attention from their teachers, ELL specialists, or others at the school.

Looking back, what could have happened to help these three students get back "on the radar"? For one thing, the teachers did not monitor students' progress across the years. Three times each year, classroom teachers used benchmark assessments of literacy to determine their students' reading levels. For example, See Sing's teacher determined that she was reading slightly below a 4th-grade level in 6th grade and documented that, by the end of the grade, she had made slight improvements. But what the 6th-grade teacher didn't know was that See Sing had been

> **Teaching Opportunity:** Older emergent bilingual students may benefit from targeted, explicit instruction and practice with specific graphophonemic relationships in English.

virtually at the same reading level for the past 3 years! Tong's 6th-grade teacher used an assessment to determine his developmental spelling stage but didn't realize that he was stuck on the same types of phonics features that had frustrated him for 4 years!

There was not a comprehensive system in place for following student progress or learning issues from year to year, which meant that each student entered each new grade level as an unknown entity to his or her teacher. Additionally, although the students received collaborative instructional support from ELL teachers along the way, those teachers were not encouraged to communicate systematically with one another or with the mainstream teachers about specific observations of student progress or concern. There was no one in the school who knew the students' personal backgrounds or development over time. No one held their whole story—only a snapshot from a given year.

One manifestation of the limited documentation of progress across the years was that students who may have been eligible for and would have benefited from special services were not identified or referred by teachers. In a conversation with the literacy coach, Ms. Casey, during the students' 6th-grade year, we asked about her impressions of the progress of Chue and Tong. She pulled out their cumulative files and downloaded their past year's scores on the MAP benchmark assessment (www.nwea.org/assessments/map/). What she saw distressed her: Both boys were many years behind their peers in reading and content areas and had shown little or no growth over 3 years. And while she knew this didn't represent their whole story, a red flag should have gone up years before so that more information could have been collected.

At Randolph Elementary, cases of students who had severe behavioral or academic difficulties typically were brought to a Teacher Assistance Team (TAT) designed to support the general education teacher by examining student data and providing support in determining next steps, including assessment for special education services in some cases. Tong and Chue had not been brought to the team, and Ms. Casey hadn't heard any concerns from classroom teachers. She hypothesized that with new Language Academy students entering their classes every year, there were always students performing below Tong and Chue, who thus were not seen as the "lowest." In a conversation with Ms. Petersen, the boys' 6th-grade teacher, she commented that they hadn't been referred to TAT because they were so new to the country. Ms. Petersen had assumed erroneously that the boys were recent immigrants because "when Chue's and Tong's families come in for conferences they're always speaking only in Hmong with each other and the children. . . . Usually our families have transitioned to using some English after a few years here." Her misperception about how long they had been learning English led her to believe that they "just needed time," when in fact they had been in the United States for many years. Although background information was accessible to teachers through the students' cumulative files, it did not appear to be common practice to consult the files. We do not know whether Chue and Tong have learning disabilities or processing issues that led to their sluggish academic growth in the intermediate grades; however, we do worry that they continued through all of elementary schooling without anyone asking the question. Ms. Casey realized, in retrospect, that the boys had slipped through the cracks and were now being sent on to middle school, where they were not likely to get the level of support they needed and likely would fall farther and farther behind.

STEPS IN THE RIGHT DIRECTION

What can school personnel do to ensure that students receive a coherent and effective program that encourages their English language development as well as their academic learning across the elementary years? This seems like a particularly daunting problem for teachers who typically work with students for only a year and then send them off to another teacher. One individual teacher will not be able to take on this issue alone. It will require the efforts of the entire school community, and possibly district personnel, to put structures and policies in place. Here are some examples of how educators can work collectively to support emergent bilinguals across the grade levels.

Professional Development to Build Staff Capacity

Perhaps one of the hardest parts for the students about transitioning to mainstream classes from their specially designed English classes was that they now spent the majority of their day with one classroom teacher who had little training on how to support emergent bilinguals. This is not true just at Randolph Elementary but also at schools across the United States. Although the number of linguistically diverse students is on the rise in classrooms, general education teachers are not fully prepared to effectively teach them. Most mainstream teachers lack basic foundational skills, knowledge, and dispositions related to ELL issues, even though as many as 88% teach ELLs (Ballantyne, Sanderman, & Levy, 2008; Karabenick & Noda, 2004).

We believe that teacher education programs as well as school districts and administrators must do better at providing teachers with the knowledge and pedagogical tools to engage in ELL-inclusive practices. Some recommendations for the professional development of inservice teachers include experiences such as:

- Ongoing co-teaching or coaching for mainstream teachers by ELL specialists with expertise and training in bilingual education
- Home and/or community visits in which teachers spend time learning from families and community members about the home languages and cultures of their students
- Release time for collaborative curriculum projects that integrate English language development standards with state content standards
- Book clubs in which teachers study professional books on the topic of emergent bilinguals (such as this one!) and participate in inquiry-based discussions

Accountability for Student Progress

As discussed in Chapter 4, one of the most important ways that teachers are able to improve student learning is by knowing their students well, which entails knowing their backgrounds and interests and also their academic growth, strengths, and weaknesses. Collecting common data points to keep track of student progress over time is essential. However, testing emergent bilingual students on disciplinary knowledge is problematic—the tests are language dependent and almost always given in English. The information that teachers receive from these tests can be misleading and have consequences for student learning.

One way that teachers can get better data about student learning is to consider multiple data sources, including students' language proficiency. We recommend gaining insight into students' oral language development through a collection of assessments on domains such as vocabulary, grammar, morphological skills, and oral comprehension (Lesaux & Marietta, 2012). These English language data used in concert with other achievement data may help provide a clearer picture of student achievement.

One source of important, but sometimes undervalued, information about oral language use is classroom observations. Teachers of emergent bilinguals need to hone their "language detective" skills in order to evaluate students' language use and growth over time. This means developing ways of collecting and analyzing students' oral and written language samples through classroom activities such as writing assignments, presentations, audio or video recordings, one-on-one conferences, and listening in on student-to-student interactions.

A Collaborative Inquiry Process

The central goal of collaborative inquiry is to engage in reflective dialogue in order to improve instruction and student learning (Saunders, Goldenberg, & Gallimore, 2009). Sometimes called professional learning communities (PLCs) or data teams, groups of teachers convene regularly and frequently during the work week with the goal of increasing student learning results. Together, teachers analyze data from a variety of sources to inform decisions about instructional planning and assessment of student learning (DuFour, 2004). PLCs have the potential to be powerful venues for looking closely at a variety of student data *over time*. Rather than examining data from the beginning of the year to the end, a PLC team could investigate information across multiple years in order to keep closer track of student growth.

Collaborative inquiry teams require time and resources as well as strong school-based leadership to keep the train on the tracks, but have great potential to improve outcomes for students learning English. If students' progress slows or if they have not acquired key skills, educators may be able to intervene to provide a learning boost. Conversely, if a student is showing growth in some areas, those strengths may be leveraged to help in others. The goal is to ensure that all students receive the high-quality instruction they need.

Inviting Families to Share Expectations

Last, although we've discussed it intensively in Chapter 5, the importance of family communication and collaboration in the effort to provide a coherent curricular program bears repeating. Three of the six students changed schools after 3rd grade because their parents were unhappy or uneasy about some aspect of their child's school experience: not being academically challenged, concerns about poor behavior, and/or lack of language and cultural connection. These parents all had specific beliefs about quality schooling for their children and felt that Randolph Elementary wasn't making the grade, so they left. The lesson here for schools is twofold: (1) Make every effort to communicate with parents about student experiences and successes; and (2) ask parents what doing well in school means to them and how to help their child achieve these goals in order to draw from family strengths and identify potential issues before it's too late. Had the teachers at Randolph Elementary had a clearer path of communication with the three discontented families, they may have been able to clarify misconceptions or make adaptations to students' learning plans.

SUMMARIZING LEARNING

Taking a wide-angle view of the elementary experiences of the six students in this book to consider the influences of their educational programs allowed us to understand more about each student's progress and challenges than a 1-year snapshot could have. The six students started in the same class with the same level of English, but ended up in different schools and different places in terms of long-term achievement. We considered how their instruction from year to year might have had an effect. We found it especially concerning that once the students entered the mainstream, many of their learning needs went undetected and "good behavior" and "trying hard" were perceived as being "enough."

Throughout the discussion you learned about programmatic approaches to teaching English learners, including specially designed instruction in English, co-teaching, and English language development, and got a peek into classrooms using these strategies. Finally, we shared some hopeful strategies for building cohesive school programs that we believe could provide a safety net for emergent bilingual students and keep them moving forward toward success in the elementary grades.

QUESTIONS FOR REFLECTION AND DISCUSSION

- What are some of the ways that teachers in your school are ensuring that emergent bilinguals continue to show progress through the elementary years?
- We use the term *specially designed instruction* to mean instruction that is not "just good teaching" but instead is designed with the unique needs of emergent bilinguals in mind. How does specially designed instruction do this? What are the practices valuable to all teachers in helping emergent bilinguals learn English and, at the same time, learn content material in English?
- Yates and Ortiz (1991) found that many teachers view linguistically diverse children as simply low-performing native English-speaking children. What are the implications of this belief? What are the differences between these groups?
- Why is it especially important to think programmatically instead of year by year when working with emergent bilingual students?

CHAPTER 7

Reflecting Back to Look Forward

In this chapter, we identify how each child's time in 1st through 6th grade highlights challenges of emergent bilinguals in their elementary years. We also reconnect with many of the big ideas that have emerged throughout the book and wrestle with the key question of what might the students encounter in secondary school and beyond. We end with a hopeful discussion about how educators can balance knowing that students need time to develop a new language with maintaining an urgency for students to learn as much as they possibly can. As you read this last chapter, stop and reflect on what you've learned about the complexities of teaching students who bring languages and background experiences that are different from standardized academic English to the classroom. Consider aspects of the students' stories that have stuck with you. Be aware of the ways that the strategies or ideas in this book have inspired you to use meaningful and effective instruction with your current or future students from linguistically diverse backgrounds. How have you learned to be a culturally relevant and sustaining teacher—one who builds upon the strengths and interests of your students, instead of fixating on what they might lack or how far behind grade-level literacy benchmarks they are?

Throughout this book, you engaged with issues that arise concerning the school language and literacy development of multilingual youth. You explored the changing context of literacy instruction in elementary school classrooms through the concrete examples of six students who learned English during their elementary school years. You observed Abdirahman, Chue, Kevin, See Sing, Tong, and Ubah negotiate languages, complex experiences, and multiple teachers in their schools. Although it is impossible to understand multilingual students' paths to literacy learning as a singular experience, a variety of individual examples can help you develop a deeper knowledge of students' challenges and successes. Looking forward, we now take a panoramic view of the literacy paths of all the students and the varied dilemmas presented in this book.

THE PATHS THROUGH ELEMENTARY SCHOOL

See Sing

> See Sing likes to read a lot and every night she likes stories so she just keeps reading and reading. Her brother and sister they don't know that much English but she has them repeat after her. She is teaching them.
>
> —See Sing's mother

Over the course of her literacy journey in elementary school, See Sing emerged as a bilingual speaker, reader, writer, and thinker of English and Hmong. According to See Sing, as the school years progressed, "it got easier." Throughout her 6 years at Randolph Elementary, See Sing adapted to not only the literacy instruction but also the social and cultural ways of being a student, a friend, a reader, a mathematician, and an artist, to name just a few of the identities she performed at school.

See Sing had a strong work ethic and it was important for her to do well at school. Still, although a few teachers mentioned their concern about her vocabulary needs and reluctance to speak up in class, in general See Sing operated "under the radar" of teachers' concerns. Perhaps for this reason, or because there were many other students who were significantly more behind than she, See Sing did not receive the extra help she needed to catch up to the grade-level expectations of her district. With regard to her school literacy achievement, her greatest challenges at the end of 6th grade included academic vocabulary and the ability to have higher level interactions around text.

Kevin

> Maggie: What does imagination mean?
> Kevin: When you create something in your mind the way you want it to be.

Kevin was asked this question during a qualitative reading assessment at the end of his 6th-grade year. Although his answer is in reference to a short text about the importance of imagination, it also embodies pieces of Kevin's elementary school story and his own imaginings of what school should be. Over the course of Kevin's primary years, he quickly progressed and made exemplary growth in reading and language. He was considered a top student in his class by 5th grade, although his disconnect from middle school in 6th grade influenced his performance in language arts class. Kevin's 6th-grade year looked very different from his 5th-grade year. We knew from Kevin's experiences in 5th grade that he was a student who cared about his learning. However, his 6th-grade teacher, Ms. Smith, held onto an unfavorable perception about who Kevin was, and ultimately this influenced Kevin's own view of who he was as a person, student, reader, and writer that year. Still, Kevin ended his 6th-grade year reading at grade level, received passing grades across the curricular areas, and passed the state standardized reading and math tests. School literacy challenges that still exist for Kevin include the acquisition of higher level vocabulary and academic motivation.

Tong

> Tong is a thinker. I think for him it really depends on how comfortable he is in a group. When he gets in a small setting he talks and talks and talks and talks.

> —Ms. Jones, 3rd-grade ELL teacher

It was important to Tong that he be *known* by the adults at school. Whenever one of our team went to the classroom, he would be the first to run over and ask, "Do I get to go with you today?" Conversations with Tong lingered and often it was his teachers or one of us who would have to cut it short. Tong was a student who learned through telling. He always had lots to tell. It was through Tong's telling that he invited adults to participate in his learning.

Tong entered 1st grade with burgeoning English language skills, seemingly ready to handle the literacy curriculum of the early grades. Still, as the years progressed Tong did not get the traction needed to make good progress in the language arts. Even though Tong participated in specially designed reading groups and received English language development instruction in both 5th and 6th grades, his progress was slow, he lacked confidence with his peers, and he was timid about participating in large groups. Tong's teachers provided support as they were able, using high-quality teaching practices and curricular materials to guide their approaches. However, at the end-of-the-year literacy/language assessment in 6th grade, he performed significantly below grade level.

A particular dilemma in Tong's journey was that nearly every year a teacher mentioned that there seemed to be something else interfering with his learning—yet no action such as a referral to speech and language or special education services was ever undertaken. In fact, he was never even brought to a discussion of a child study team at the school. As Mr. Parks, the 6th-grade ELL teacher at Randolph Elementary, shared, "Tong's language is hindered by something, which I don't think is fully understood by the people who work with him." Tong's story presents a significant concern for us: We certainly don't have all the answers for what could have been done to help him; however, we know that school personnel did not adequately assess and address what had gotten him stuck.

Abdirahman

A very kindhearted young man who loves to learn.

—Ms. Abdullah, Abdirahman's 6th-grade teacher

Abdirahman came to 1st grade at Randolph Elementary eager to learn all that he could about school. Beginning that year, he frequently was mesmerized by the content in lessons and engaging socially with his teachers and peers. He was a deep thinker and hard worker, and genuinely liked school. Because his enthusiasm for school often was demonstrated in ways his primary teachers thought of as noncompliant behaviors (e.g., not raising his hand to answer questions), they focused more on his behavior than his skills. With the role model of his older brother and the steady guidance of his mother, he showed exemplary language growth and used language to solve problems. Abdirahman proved to be self-motivated and was determined to read interesting books and write about content he learned. At the end of the elementary journey he was reading at grade level, although some higher level vocabulary words continued to hinder him. Abdirahman highlights for us that in order to keep developing academic language proficiency, even enthusiastic and high-performing emergent bilinguals need guidance in slowing down complex language and analyzing its meaning and usage. Only with this support will learners acquire the language of complex academic content.

Chue

I just think it will take him more time. Chue works hard. I think Chue will be okay going into 4th grade. He is not afraid to ask questions when he is stuck. He knows he is below grade level but it doesn't stop him. There are no confidence issues.

—3rd-grade ELL teacher

Chue's elementary teachers' overall sense of him was that he was savvy socially, but not academically. All in all, many teachers didn't seem to be concerned about Chue's academic progress although he continued to perform far below grade-level expectations. As he left elementary school, his teachers described him as a confident student with the skills necessary to persist.

By the end of 6th grade, his reading was almost 3 years below grade level. Chue's slower acquisition of English language proficiency, coupled with his struggles to gain foundational literacy skills, created a tension between the time he needed to develop a new language and the time that existed for him to meet grade-level literacy benchmarks. A major issue that challenged Chue was the cross-linguistic sound confusion between Hmong and English. His verbal engagement in class, essential to language development, was always limited. In a similar manner to Tong, we saw that Chue did not receive the depth of assessment that might have led to more focused instructional support. Chue was a student who would likely benefit from a school setting that had a well-developed structure of multitiered systems of support. In such a system, Chue would be identified as someone who needed extra support, and his progress would be monitored in a regular manner. Chue needed an intensity of oversight through his early years that he did not receive.

Ubah

> She always prefers to go to the library to get help with her homework. She gets help from one of the library staff. Then after that, after she finishes her homework, she uses the computer.

> —Ubah's mother, 1st grade

Ubah showed steady progress each year and met or closely approached grade-level benchmarks. Her disposition toward learning during her elementary years can be described as buoyant. Her parents actively exercised their agency to find a more challenging curriculum and school setting, and Ubah eventually attended a suburban public school. Although Ubah changed schools three times, she was able to ride through these changes with very little impact on her learning. She plateaued for a while in 5th grade, then improved again in 6th grade, and finished at a 6th-grade reading level. In 6th grade she was officially exited from being considered an ELL student in the school system. Ubah was still challenged, however, by academic vocabulary and higher level interactions around text as she prepared to enter middle school.

BEYOND ELEMENTARY SCHOOL

As we spent time with the six students featured in this book, we witnessed their physical, emotional, and cognitive development throughout the grade levels and across various school settings. Despite their maturation, we wondered whether secondary school would be a precipitous transition for them. The 7th- through 12th-grade school experience in the United States requires more independence on the part of students and an increase in the number of teachers that students see each day, thus creating a less cohesive environment. Were the students ready for the impersonal and fast-paced environment of secondary schooling in the United States? Or, more important, were secondary school personnel ready to welcome and build on these students' capabilities?

Three of the students we followed could be considered at or close to grade level in their reading at the end of 6th grade. Three others were behind or significantly behind. All of the students were challenged by higher level academic vocabulary and complex sentence structures, and this language constraint affected both their reading comprehension and writing skills. Given what we know about the dense content focus and limited support for literacy interventions in secondary schools for students aspiring to become independent readers, we are left to wonder about what awaits them.

At the end of the 6th-grade year, we interviewed the students' teachers and asked them about the transition to middle school/junior high. Teachers of the three highest performing students, Abdirahman, Kevin, and Ubah, felt that the students would likely be successful. The teachers of the three long-term English learners expressed serious concerns. Mr. Parks, the ELL teacher, said:

> I think junior high is tough developmentally for those kids. It is not structured in a way that is best for them. They need to have strong resolution and the ability to maintain their own focus on their own goals.

Mr. Parks and Ms. Petersen, the 6th-grade teacher, pointed out that all three of these students were frequently quiet during whole-group instruction, although they did participate more in small-group settings and socializing with their friends. However, Mr. Parks and Ms. Petersen pointed out that more academic language and complicated, or "heavy," topics would be a challenge for all three students. Although all of the students' 6th-grade teachers noted some progress from the beginning of the year in reading and writing, they pointed to the growing gap between these students' academic performance and the grade-level expectations.

The consequences for secondary students who aren't academically successful can be dire. English learners are about twice as likely to drop out as native and fluent English speakers (Callahan, 2013), and the longer students are classified as ELL, the greater the likelihood that they will drop out of school (Kim, 2011). Mr. Parks noted that although the three students were "sweet and thoughtful," there was the potential for getting "swept into a spiral and out of control"—finding themselves getting involved in bad social scenes in their communities, including local gangs. "There are a lot of gangs out there, tons of them. I have seen such nice kids get sucked in. That worries me," he said.

TURNING DILEMMAS INTO DIFFERENTIATED OPPORTUNITIES

A primary goal in writing this book was to illuminate the complexities of structuring successful learning environments for linguistically diverse elementary students. We hope that you have wrestled with the dilemmas throughout this book in the same way they were intended—not to make you feel hopeless, but to spark you to be thoughtful and ready to tackle challenges when you meet students with similar stories in your own classroom. We hope we have shared the great respect we have for the students, their families, and the hard-working teachers we have introduced throughout this book. But now is the time to put your learning into action.

In the upcoming section, we vault from the dilemmas in order to revisit some of the key ideas for action that we have shared, moving from specific instructional tasks within the classroom to broader and more holistic support structures for families.

Knowing and Being Known

In several of the chapters, we explored the big idea of knowing individual students and their families more deeply. We have emphasized the importance of getting to know students, their families, and their home languages and cultures. This knowledge gives you the power to connect out-of-school experiences to learning in the classroom.

You learned that the demographic divide between teachers and students from different cultural and discourse communities has an impact on your communication with students, your interpretation of students' behaviors, and the ways in which you are able to understand or connect your own schooling and lived experiences to the experiences of your students. In response, you can explore *ways of knowing* your students: moving beyond "just teach" teacher relationships; providing instrumental support; and engaging a benefit-of-the-doubt treatment of students (Chhuon & Wallace, 2012). Exploring ways of knowing offers up possibilities for you to think deeply about how to build relationships with students and support an approach that Rosalie Rolón-Dow (2005) calls critical care, which takes into consideration the broader social-political context of their lives.

The principles of culturally relevant teaching and family involvement suggest that all of the students we observed could have benefited from more explicit connections between their home cultures and their school experiences. The focus of the specially designed Language Academy classroom was to help students attain basic English language skills while making connections to their home languages and cultures. While the students felt very comfortable in choosing to speak to one another in their home languages or English, teachers often were unaware of what the students actually were talking about in their home languages. You have opportunities every day to make these connections with students. Creating meaningful family engagement also means assisting families with access to resources beyond the school walls.

Connecting with Out-of-School Resources

Out-of-school time and out-of-school opportunities are areas that you can tap when you work with students who are not acquiring English as fast as academic standards outline. Out-of-school time includes what happens in the home, but also what opportunities are available to the students and families after school or within the community. Chue would have been a good candidate for home tutoring or out-of-school support such as tutoring at a public library or community center. School personnel need to link families to community resources that exist to support students closer to their homes. As a teacher working with students who must learn language and content at the same time, research what resources might be available to your students. While taking this step requires a bit of effort at the beginning, the results in students' growth can reward you throughout the year.

Differentiation

Throughout this book we explored the academic literacy and language trajectories of the focal students. In our years of observation, we found many great practices that helped students to surge ahead in their English literacy skills, and we also found missed opportunities or missing information. For example, students such as See Sing, who were quiet and displayed compliant school behaviors, often hovered below the radar when it came to their academic needs. The opposite may have been true as well; Abdirahman was energetic, talkative, and curious, and his school behaviors often were seen as a detriment rather than an asset. Behind his loud, gruff voice and active body was a drive for learning. His proclivity for learning language could have been capitalized on in a number of ways by teachers through the years.

Differentiation is not just for below-benchmark students but also to challenge or engage students who are on their own course. With students like Abdirahman, consider ways to inspire them, such as through project-based learning or self-selected research. Rote instruction and expectations for seat-based learning do not offer much challenge to learners. Ubah also had a great big personality that teachers read in different ways. Her strong oral English skills often misled teachers about her real abilities within the grade-level curriculum. In Ubah's 6th-grade year, her language arts teacher in a suburban middle school hadn't had much experience with English learners and assumed that Ubah was doing fine. Ubah was doing well, but she could have been challenged to do better with an individualized approach.

Oral Language Practice

One of the most straightforward ways for emergent bilinguals to expand and solidify their English skills is to practice using them. There are some simple ways to begin to help emergent bilinguals practice their English during the school day. Here are some things for you to try:

- Build in more time for oral language practice by structuring explicit opportunities for students to speak with others in English.
- Ensure that artifacts and reference materials support conversation on academic topics.
- Create opportunities to have one-on-one conversations with emergent bilingual students, especially those who are shy.
- Collect data that you can use for later targeted language instruction.

Communication Across Classrooms and Grade Levels

In Chapter 6 we took a wide-angle view of how schools monitor the development of language and literacy across the elementary years. While some procedures and policies were in place within schools and districts to support a smooth delivery of services to children, in retrospect we identified many gaps in documentation. Particularly challenging were times of transition, such as when students returned to school in the fall or when there was a change in program placement.

Two of the students we observed were transitioned out of their specially designed language classroom early. Ubah's mother advocated for this, and Ubah's advanced social and verbal skills made this seem like a good decision. Her parents also believed that being "mainstreamed" would lead her to be more challenged, but that wasn't the case initially. See Sing also was transitioned early but struggled to keep up with grade-level benchmarks. Because she was well behaved in the classroom, her literacy skills were not closely examined from year to year.

What procedures for documenting student learning do you have in place at your school, or might you suggest to your staff? You can work to make student progress a collaborative expectation across grade levels and throughout students' whole tenure at your site. Documenting student success (or lack thereof) is a powerful motivator for continuous school improvement and will help you feel a sense of shared responsibility and achievement within your school learning community.

Power of Bilingualism

One of the ways elementary teachers can improve students' self-confidence and perhaps academic success is to celebrate the power of bilingualism with them. Bilingualism and biliteracy carry many cognitive benefits for students, as well as the potential for enhanced career options (Rodríguez et al., 2014). In all of our interviews, parents stressed the cultural value of raising bilingual children. You can encourage your students to explore more options by acknowledging their developing bilingualism and being supportive of their home language skills. Encourage parents to talk extensively and deeply on various topics using their home languages. Set the tone in your classroom for celebrating the notion of becoming or being bilingual.

Urgency

It takes time to develop academic English for emergent bilinguals. Still, time is not enough. For example, Chue had spent his entire elementary career at Randolph and yet was assumed by some of his teachers to be a recent immigrant because of his emergent-level English language skills. As you come to learn more about your students, their cultural and linguistic backgrounds, and their academic journeys, you can strive to hold high yet achievable expectations. The specific practices we have suggested throughout this book will help, but the urgency must start with you.

CONCLUSION

At the beginning of this book we described a story cloth from the Hmong culture and connected it to See Sing and her family's journey into U.S. schools. We considered how the cloth was intertwined with a series of personal and community experiences, just as a person's literacy is woven tightly with language and identity. Through the words in this book, you have traveled with See Sing and five other emergent bilingual students on their language and literacy journeys. On the way, you've seen ups and downs and explored ways to create better pathways for your own future students. We close with the hope that See Sing's mother expressed for her children, that they "study hard" and "do what my heart wishes for them." We echo her wishes for you, the reader. Teach with all your effort. Listen to your students and come to know them. Build bridges to connect what they bring to the rigorous academic expectations you can help them attain. In this way you will join them on the path of learning.

Glossary

Academic Language: The language needed for students to understand complex texts and participate in school learning.

Academic Language Proficiency: The ability to construct meaning from oral language and written texts, relate complex ideas and information, recognize features of different genres, and use a variety of linguistic strategies to communicate (Dutro & Moran, 2003).

Academic Language Objective: Identification and articulation of the academic language functions and skills that learners need to master to fully participate in the lesson and meet the grade-level content standards.

African American English: A variation of English spoken within African American communities of the United States.

Bidirectional Family Engagement: Interaction between schools and students' families that is reciprocal. It includes actions taken by school personnel that help to support families.

Code Mesh: To insert words or phrases from more than one language or dialect with purpose.

Cognates: Words that have similar spellings and meanings across languages as *air* (English) and *aire* (Spanish).

Collaborative instruction: A teaching method that allows two teachers with different areas of expertise to work together, often in one classroom, to meet the needs of the students.

Culture: The social practices of people in a community. It encompasses ways of being, the forms of interactions, and the norms, values, and practices of communication that people use to interact and be recognized. It is important to remember that culture is fluid, not something fixed or rigid.

Cultural Capital: A term first used by sociologist Pierre Bourdieu (1977). Cultural capital includes sociocultural resources, such as language and education, that people draw upon to participate successfully within society.

Culturally Relevant Pedagogy (CRP): A teaching theory used to effectively provide academic support and build relationships with students from diverse backgrounds. CRP is a pedagogical framework that recognizes the community and home cultures of students and integrates students' funds of knowledge into the everyday classroom.

Culturally Sustaining Pedagogy (CSP): Teaching that builds from asset-based pedagogies and aims to cultivate linguistic, literate, and cultural pluralism in schools; respond to local and global population shifts toward a majority multilingual society; and create opportunities for social change and transformation in public schools (Paris, 2012).

Decoding Skills: The ability to apply knowledge of letter–sound relationships to correctly pronounce written words.

Demographic Divide: The disparities in race, language, culture, and economic background between the student and teacher populations in the United States.

Discourse Communities: Discourse includes the ways people use language, gain understanding, and act in order to be recognized socially by members of a community (Gee, 2014). A Discourse community is a group of people who share some purpose for interacting and use language in specific ways to do so. Individuals are a part of multiple discourse communities, for example, elementary education teacher, Spanish speaker, sports team member, female or male, White, and middle class. Discourse communities form the ways we come to understand things and shape what we call our identity.

Emergent Bilingual: A student who brings a non-English home language to school and learns English there. An emergent bilingual is gaining English proficiency along with home language proficiency, thereby becoming bilingual.

English Learner or **English Language Learner:** A student who is in the process of learning English as a new language. We make an effort to avoid this term because it positions the student as "lacking" in ability, rather than highlighting that he or she is becoming bilingual.

Family Engagement: The ways that families assist with school and classroom activities, including preparing children for school, supporting schoolwork, and attending conferences.

Funds of Knowledge: The background experiences, languages, communicative competence, interests, histories, family support, and so much more that students bring to the classroom. These strengths help students to understand the academic world from their own perspective and make the most of it.

Inflection: An alteration to the format of a base word (usually marked by an affix at the end of the word) that expresses grammatical meaning. In the Hmong language, words are not inflected as they are in English and Spanish.

Instrumental Support: Providing concrete ways to reinforce or structure student learning.

Language Academy: One district's special program designed to provide students who are new to the country and/or who have very low English proficiency levels with intensive English language development, grade-level content, and an opportunity to participate in general education classrooms for part of the school day for a two-year period.

Lexicon: The total stock of words and word elements that carry *meaning* in a language, an individual speaker or group of speakers, or a subject.

Linguistically Diverse Student: A student who brings a home language other than standardized academic English to school. Linguistically diverse students may speak English as a first language; however, it may be a variation of English that is different from the language used in schooling (e.g., African American English or Spanish-influenced English).

Long-Term English Learners: Students who remain categorized as English learners in school and find themselves "stuck" in ELL classes in secondary schools even though they've been in the United States for many years.

Metalinguistic Awareness: A reflective practice that involves thinking about language structure, function, and use in general.

Migrant: A person who moves from place to place to get work.

Morphology: The way words are constructed using meaningful chunks such as *non* + *smoke* +*er* (a person who doesn't smoke).

Multilingual Student: A student who operates in various languages or dialects throughout his or her life in and out of school. Students use more than one language to interact with friends, family, church members, and/or the community, and transition across these discourse communities.

Newcomer: A term used within schools that identifies transnational students who have the least English proficiency and/or are new immigrants to the United States. Newcomer students may be placed in newcomer programs that aim to meet the academic and transitional needs of newly arrived immigrant children by providing specially designed instruction in which students learn academic content and language at the same time (U.S. Department of Education, 1999).

Pedagogical Content Knowledge: Knowledge gathered in courses and prior teaching experiences about instruction in a particular content area.

Pragmatics: Aspects of language that go beyond the words, such as proximity of speaking, what is considered polite, eye contact, etc.

Professional Learning Community (PLC): A small team of teachers in a school who work collectively on issues of student learning and improving teaching practice.

Subtle Aspects of Parental Involvement: A term coined by Jeynes (2010). These aspects create an "academically oriented" home where families spend quality time talking about school and what is being learned.

Syntax: How words are put together into phrases and sentences.

Tonal Languages: Languages that use tones to differentiate the meaning of words. Examples of tonal languages include Hmong and Mandarin Chinese.

Transnational Student (or Family): A student who has ties across national borders either because the family immigrated to the United States or because there is an ongoing family relationship with people or places in other countries. These connections also may take shape in relationships in the United States with fellow immigrants from specific geographical regions.

Two-Generation Approach: An approach that involves families and children working together on activities that promote student literacy development. At the school level, educational personnel are encouraged to help parents learn about two-generation approaches they can use at home with their children.

Unidirectional Family Engagement: Practices that focus on what families can do to support school goals and students' academic achievement. It does not address what school communities and staff can do to work collaboratively with families.

About the Research Study

We began our study in collaboration with an urban school district, a group of 1st-grade students, their teachers, and their parents. Our goal was to document the children's language and literacy learning through elementary school, grades 1–6. During the longitudinal study, we posed questions such as: What types of experiences did these emergent bilinguals have during their elementary years? How did these experiences contribute to or hinder students' school achievement?

Overview

From 2006–2012 we collected data from the following sources: (a) annual structured family interviews; (b) artifacts of student literacy development such as writing, spelling, and reading samples; (c) structured classroom observations and student interviews; (d) assessment data on language proficiency, reading level and proficiency, and developmental spelling stage; and (e) annual structured interviews with teachers to triangulate data on the students' language and literacy progress.

Procedures

Lori was the primary investigator for this study, and Carrie, Amy, and Maggie each served 2 years as research assistants. We spent time collecting observational data in the classroom, focusing on the literacy activities students participated in; the language they used in their work with peers or adults; their level of engagement; and what they chose to read and write. We collected a total of nine observations per student over each school year during whole-group, small-group, and independent work times in class.

Annually we conducted family interviews that were recorded and later transcribed. The family interview, conducted in the home or in the community, informed our understanding of the values the families held for their children, perceptions of their children's language development, attitudes toward schooling, and literacy activities in the home. Lori conducted the interviews with Spanish-speaking family members, and interpreters from the school or community assisted with the Hmong and Somali families.

Yearly interviews with each student's teacher were conducted in the classroom to reflect with teachers about how they organized their day, insights they had about the focus student's learning, and how they saw the student interacting socially in class. Teachers shared impressions of the focus students' strengths or challenges in language and literacy development.

Measures

To document the students' literacy journey, we collected writing, spelling, and oral reading samples throughout the year. We used the oral component of the Language Assessment Scales (LAS-O) at the beginning and end of the school year (De Avila & Duncan, 1994). The LAS-O measure provided a standardized score of students' familiarity with common school vocabulary as well as allowed us to take a pre/post sample of their English-listening comprehension through an oral story retell.

We used qualitative spelling inventories from *Words Their Way* (Bear et al., 2012) three times a year. When taking the spelling inventory, students were given the words individually and within a sentence. We used established guidelines for identifying a developmental spelling stage for each student. We analyzed each student's understanding of the English-writing system and how their home language might influence their phonetic representations.

To gather information about students' reading growth, we began by collecting data in the early years related to (a) phonemic awareness skills such as hearing initial sounds in words, blending, and segmenting sounds, (b) letter and letter-sound knowledge, and (c) sight-word knowledge. We administered informal reading inventories two to three times per year using an informal reading inventory or a similar set of passages used by the school to document students' fluency and comprehension behaviors and identify an approximate grade level for their reading. Once students were reading at an intermediate level, we would ask them to read from a text they were using at independent reading time, to observe their reading behaviors.

Three times a year we collected a prompted writing sample that served the dual purpose of being both a writing sample and an artifact of their oral language. We provided a prompt such as, "Share about going to the market with your family," and asked students to draw a picture and write words or sentences to tell their story. We recorded students reading their narratives and followed up by having a conversation that extended the topic. We transcribed these interactions and analyzed the samples for students' vocabulary use and the syntactic difficulty of their discourse.

References

American Association of Colleges of Nursing. (2008). The essentials of baccalaureate education for professional nursing practice. Washington, DC: Author.

Appleby, J., Brinkley, A., McPherson, J., & Broussard, A. (2003). *The American vision* (3rd ed.). New York, NY: Glencoe/McGraw-Hill.

Arias, M. B., & Morillo-Campbell, M. (2008). Promoting ELL parental involvement: Challenges in contested times. Tempe, AZ: Education Policy Research Unit, Arizona State University. Retrieved from epsl.asu.edu/epru/documents/EPSL -0801-250-EPRU.pdf

Audet, T. I., Gibson, K., & Flag, A. (1995). A treasure chest of life. *The Mailbox, 17*(2), 26–33.

Bailey, A. L., & Osipova, A. V. (2015). Children's multilingual development and education: Fostering linguistic resources in home and school contexts. New York, NY: Cambridge University Press.

Ballantyne, K. G., Sanderman, A. R., & Levy, J. (2008). *Educating English language learners: Building teacher capacity* (Roundtable Report). Washington, DC: National Clearinghouse for English Language Acquisition & Language Instruction Educational Programs.

Bear, D. R., Invernizzi, M., Templeton, S., & Johnston, F. (2012). *Words their way: Word study for phonics, vocabulary, and spelling instruction* (5th ed.). Boston, MA: Pearson/Allyn & Bacon.

Bear, D. R., Invernizzi, M., Templeton, S., & Johnston, F. (2016). *Words their way: Word study for phonics, vocabulary, and spelling instruction* (6th ed.). Boston, MA: Pearson.

Bourdieu, P. (1977). Cultural reproduction and social reproduction In J. Karabel & A. H. Halsey (Eds.), *Power and ideology in education.* (pp. 487–511). New York, NY: Oxford University Press.

California Commission on Teacher Credentialing. (2009). *California Standards for the Teaching Profession (CSTP).* Sacramento: California Department of Education.

Callahan, R. M. (2013). *The English learner dropout dilemma: Multiple risks and multiple resources.* Santa Barbara: University of California, Santa Barbara, California Dropout Research Project.

Cannon, J. (2008). *Stellaluna.* New York, NY: Scholastic.

Center for Research on Education, Diversity & Excellence. (2001, September). *Some program alternatives for English language learners.* Retrieved from crede .berkeley.edu/products/print/pract_briefs/pb3.shtml

Chhuon, V., & Wallace, T. L. (2012). Creating connectedness through being known: Fulfilling the need to belong in U.S. high schools. *Youth and Society, 46*(3), 379–401.

Collier, V. P., & Thomas, W. P. (2004). The astounding effectiveness of dual language education for all. *NABE Journal of Research and Practice, 2*(1), 1–20.

Costello, R. W. (1987). Improving student achievement by overcoming teacher isolation. *The Clearing House, 61*(2), 91–94.

Council of Chief State School Officers. (2011). *Interstate Teacher Assessment and Support Consortium (InTASC) Model Core Teaching Standards: A resource for state dialogue.* Washington, DC: Author.

Creese, A., & Martin, P. (Eds.). (2003). *Multilingual classroom ecologies: Interrelationships, interactions, and ideologies.* Buffalo, NY: Multilingual Matters.

Cummins, J. (2000). *Language, power, and pedagogy: Bilingual children in the crossfire* (Vol. 23). New York, NY: Multilingual Matters.

De Avila, D., & Duncan, S. (1994) Language Assessment Scales–Oral (LAS-O). Monterey, CA: CTB Macmillan/McGraw-Hill.

Delgado Gaitan, C. (2012). Culture, literacy, and power in family–community–school–relationships. *Theory Into Practice, 51*, 305–311.

Dove, M., & Honigsfeld, A. (2010). ESL coteaching and collaboration: Opportunities to develop teacher leadership and enhance student learning. *TESOL Journal, 1*(1), 3–22.

DuFour, R. (2004). What is a "professional learning community"? *Educational Leadership, 61*(8), 6–11.

Dunn, L., & Dunn, D. (2007). *Peabody picture vocabulary test* (4th ed.). Boston, MA: Pearson.

Dutro, S., & Moran, C. (2003). Rethinking English language instruction: An architectural approach. In G. G. Garcia (Ed.), *English learners: Reaching the highest level of English literacy* (pp. 227–258). Newark, DE: International Reading Association.

Dutro, S., Núñez, R., & Helman, L. (2016). Explicit language instruction: A key to academic success for English learners. In L. Helman (Ed.), *Literacy development with English learners: Research-based instruction in grades K–6* (2nd ed.). New York, NY: Guilford Press.

Ferdman, B. (1990). Literacy and cultural identity. *Harvard Educational Review, 60*(2), 181–205.

Francis, D., Lesaux, N., & August, D. (2006). Language of instruction. In D. August & T. Shanahan (Eds.), *Developing literacy in second-language learners: Report of The National Literacy Panel on Language–Minority Children and Youth* (pp. 365–413). Mahwah, NJ: Lawrence Erlbaum.

Frederick, A. R. (2013). A case study of a first-grade teacher team collaboratively planning literacy instruction for English learners. Retrieved from purl.umn.edu/155719

Friend, M. (2008). Co-teaching: A simple solution that isn't simple after all. *Journal of Curriculum and Instruction, 2*(2), 9–19.

Gee, J. P. (2014). *An Introduction to Discourse Analysis: Theory and Method.* New York, NY: Routledge.

Genesee, F., Lindholm-Leary, K., Saunders, W., & Christian, D. (2006). *Educating English language learners.* New York, NY: Cambridge University Press.

Genishi, C., & Dyson, A. H. (2009). *Children, language, and literacy: Diverse learners in diverse times*. New York, NY: Teachers College Press.

Good, M., Masewicz, S., & Vogel, L. (2010). Latino English language learners: Bridging achievement and cultural gaps between schools and families. *Journal Of Latinos & Education, 9*(4), 321–339.

Goodwin, A. L., & King, S. H. (2002). *Culturally responsive parental involvement: Concrete understandings and basic strategies*. Washington, DC: American Association of Colleges for Teacher Education.

Grosjean, F. (2010). *Bilingual: Life and reality*. Cambridge, MA: Harvard University Press.

Hakuta, K., Butler, Y. G., & Witt, D. (2000). How long does it take English learners to attain proficiency? (Policy Report 2000-1). Santa Barbara, CA: University of California Linguistic Minority Research Institute.

Helman, L. (2004). Building on the sound system of Spanish: Insights from the alphabetic spellings of English language learners. *The Reading Teacher, 57*, 452–460.

Helman, L. A. (2005). Spanish speakers learning to read in English: What a large-scale assessment suggests about their progress. In B. Maloch, J. Hoffman, D. Schallert, C. Fairbanks, & J. Worthy (Eds.), *54th Yearbook of the National Reading Conference* (pp. 211–226). Oak Creek, WI: National Reading Conference.

Helman, L. (2009). Literacy development with English learners: Research-based instruction in grades K–6. New York, NY: Guilford Press.

Helman, L., Bear, D. R., Invernizzi, M., Templeton, S., & Johnston, F. (2009). *Letter-name alphabetic sorts for Spanish-speaking English learners*. Boston, MA: Pearson.

Henderson, E. H. (1981). *Learning to read and spell: The child's knowledge of words*. DeKalb: Northern Illinois University Press.

Heritage, M. (2013). Formative assessment in practice: A process of inquiry and action. Cambridge, MA: Harvard Education Press.

Israel, M., & Arbus, D. (2011). *Diane Arbus: An Aperture monograph*. Millerton, NY: Aperture.

Jeynes, W. (2010). The salience of the subtle aspects of parental involvement and encouraging that involvement: Implications for school-based programs. *Teachers College Record, 112*(3), 747–774.

Jiménez, R. T. (2000). Literacy and the identity development of Latina/o students. *American Educational Research Journal, 37*(4), 971–1000.

Jiménez, R. T., & Rose, B. C. (2010). Knowing how to know: Building meaningful relationships through instruction that meets the needs of students learning English. *Journal of Teacher Education, 61*(5), 403–412.

Kalantzis, M., Cope, B., & Harvey, A. (2003). Assessing multiliteracies and the new basics. *Assessment in Education, 10*(1), 15–26.

Karabenick, S. A., & Noda, P.A.C. (2004). Professional development implications of teachers' beliefs and attitudes toward English language learners. *Bilingual Research Journal, 28*, 55–75.

Kids Count Data Center. (2013). Fourth graders who scored below proficient reading by English language learner status. Retrieved from datacenter.kidscount.org

Kim, J. (2011). *Relationships among and between ELL status, demographic characteristics, enrollment history, and school persistence* (CRESST Report 810). Los Angeles, CA: National Center for Research on Evaluation, Standards, and Student Testing.

Knoblauch, C. H. (1990). Literacy and the politics of education. In A. A. Lumsford, H. Moglen, & J. Slevin (Eds.), *The right to literacy* (pp. 74–80). New York, NY: Modern Language Association of America.

Ladson-Billings, G. (1995). Toward a theory of culturally relevant pedagogy. *American educational research journal, 32*(3), 465–491.

Lee & Low Books. (2013). *Classroom guide for Dia's story cloth.* Retrieved from https://www.leeandlow.com/books/2385/teachers_guide

Lenski, S., Mack, C. L., & Brown, J. E. (2008). Critical elements for literacy instruction of teacher candidates for urban settings. In L. C. Wilkinson, L. M. Morrow, & V. Chou (Eds.), *Improving literacy achievement in urban schools: Critical elements in teacher preparation.* (pp. 61–80). Newark, DE: International Reading Association.

Lesaux, N. K., & Geva, E. (2006). Synthesis: Development of literacy in language-minority students. In D. August & T. Shanahan (Eds.), *Developing literacy in second-language learners* (pp. 53–74). Mahwah, NJ: Erlbaum.

Lesaux, N. K., & Marietta, S. H. (2012). Making assessment matter: Using test results to differentiate reading instruction. New York, NY: Guilford Press.

McGinn, F., & McMenamin, J. (1984). *Acquiring English: An ESL teacher's guide for the Hmong student.* Los Angeles: California State University, Los Angeles.

Menken, K., Kleyn, T., & Chae, N. (2012). Spotlight on "long-term English language learners": Characteristics and prior schooling experiences of an invisible population. *International Multilingual Research Journal, 6*(2), 121–142.

Moll, L. C., Amanti, C., Neff, D., & Gonzalez, N. (1992). Funds of knowledge for teaching: Using a qualitative approach to connect homes and classrooms. *Theory into Practice, 31,* 132–141.

Moll, L. C., & González, N. (1994). Critical issues: Lessons from research with language-minority children. *Journal of Reading Behavior, 26*(4), 439–457.

Mondo Educational Publishing. (2015). *Let's talk about it!* [Kit D]. New York, NY: Author.

Nagy, W., & Townsend, D. (2012). Words as tools: Learning academic vocabulary as language acquisition. *Reading Research Quarterly, 47*(1), 91–108.

National Board for Professional Teaching Standards. (2012). *Literacy: Reading–language arts standards* (2nd ed.). San Antonio, TX: NBPTS Processing Center.

National Governors Association Center for Best Practices & Council of Chief State School Officers. (2010). Common core state standards for English language arts and literacy in history/social studies, science, and technical subjects. Washington, DC: Authors.

Northwest Evaluation Association. (2011). *Measures of academic progress: Reading.* Portland, OR: Author.

Paris, D. (2012). Culturally sustaining pedagogy: A needed change in stance, terminology, and practice. *Educational Researcher, 41*(3), 93–97.

Paris, D., & Alim, H. S. (2014). What are we seeking to sustain through culturally sustaining pedagogy? A loving critique forward. *Harvard Educational Review, 84*(1), 85–100.

Pearson, P. D. (2007). A historical analysis of the impact of educational research on policy and practice: Reading as an illustrative case. In D. W. Rowe, R. T. Jiménez, D. L. Compton, D. K. Dickinson., Y. Kim, K. M. Leander, & V. J. Risko (Eds.), *56th Yearbook of the National Reading Conference* (pp. 14–40). Oak Creek, WI: National Reading Conference.

Peregoy, S. F., & Boyle, O. F. (2012). *Reading, writing and learning in ESL: A resource book for teaching K–12 English learners* (6th ed.). Boston, MA: Pearson.

Rodríguez, D., Carrasquillo, A., & Lee, K. S. (2014). *The bilingual advantage: Promoting academic development, biliteracy, and native language in the classroom.* New York, NY: Teachers College Press.

Rolón-Dow, R. (2005). Critical care: A color (full) analysis of care narratives in the schooling experiences of Puerto Rican girls. *American Educational Research Journal, 42*(1), 77–111.

Rose, S., & Schimke, K. (2012). *Third grade literacy policies: Identification, intervention, retention.* Denver, CO: Education Commission of the States. Retrieved from www.ecs.org/clearinghouse/01/01/54/10154.pdf

Ross, T. (2015). The Case for a Two-Generation Approach for Educating English Language Learners. Washington, DC: Center for American Progress. Retrieved from cdn.americanprogress.org/wp-content/uploads/2015/05/Ross-ELL-report.pdf

Ryan, C. (2013). *Language use in the United States: 2011* (American Community Survey Reports). Washington, DC: U.S. Department of Commerce/U.S. Census Bureau.

Samson, J. F., & Collins, B. A. (2012). *Preparing all teachers to meet the needs of English language learners.* Washington, DC: Center for American Progress.

Saunders, W. M., Goldenberg, C. N., & Gallimore, R. (2009). Increasing achievement by focusing grade-level teams on improving classroom learning: A prospective, quasi-experimental study of Title I schools. *American Educational Research Journal, 46*(4), 1006–1033.

Saunders, W., Goldenberg, C., & Marcelletti, D. (2013). English language development: Guidelines for instruction. *American Educator, 37*(2), 13.

Saunders, W. M., & O'Brien, G. (2006). Oral language. In F. Genesee, K. Lindholm-Leary, W. M. Saunders, & D. Christian (Eds.), *Educating English learners: A synthesis of research evidence* (pp. 14–63). Cambridge, UK: Cambridge University Press.

Scarborough, H. S. (2001). Connecting early language and literacy to later reading (dis)abilities: Evidence, theory, and practice. In S. B. Neuman & D. K. Dickinson (Eds.), *Handbook of early literacy research* (pp. 97–110). New York, NY: Guilford Press.

Shatz, M., & Wilkinson, L. C. (2010). *The education of English language learners: Research to practice.* New York, NY: Guilford Press.

Slavin, R., & Cheung, A. (2005). A synthesis of research on language of reading instruction for English language learners. *Review of Educational Research, 75*(2), 247–284.

Strive Together Network. (2015). Vision/road map. See strivetogether.org/vision-roadmap

Tutwiler, S. W. (2005). *Teachers as collaborative partners: Working with diverse families and communities.* Mahwah, NJ: Lawrence Erlbaum Associates.

U.S. Department of Education, Office of English Language Acquisition. (2015). English learner tool kit. Retrieved from www2.ed.gov/about/offices/list/oela/english-learner-toolkit/index.html

Valdés, G. (2001). *Learning and not learning English: Latino students in American schools.* New York, NY: Teachers College Press.

Valenzuela, A. (1999). *Subtractive schooling: US-Mexican youth and the politics of caring.* Albany: State University of New York Press.

Williams, L., Roberts, M., Roberts, L., & Corrigan, E. (1986). *The little old lady who was not afraid of anything.* New York, NY: Harper Collins.

Yamamoto, Y., & Holloway, S. D. (2010). Parental expectations and children's academic performance in sociocultural context. *Educational Psychology Review, 22*(3), 189–214

Yates, J. R., & Ortiz, A. A. (1991). Professional development needs of teachers who serve exceptional language minorities in today's schools. *Teacher Education and Special Education: The Journal of the Teacher Education Division of the Council for Exceptional Children, 14*(1), 11–18.

York-Barr, J., Ghere, G., & Sommerness, J. (2007). Collaborative teaching to increase ELL student learning: A three-year urban elementary case study. *Journal of Education for Students Placed at Risk, 12*(3), 301–335.

Index

The letter *f* or *t* following a page number indicates a figure or table, respectively.

About the Authors

Lori Helman, PhD, is associate professor at the University of Minnesota in the Department of Curriculum and Instruction and director of the Minnesota Center for Reading Research. She specializes in literacy education for preservice and graduate students and works closely with elementary schools to implement schoolwide approaches to curricular reform. Formerly an elementary bilingual classroom teacher, she was also coordinator of beginning teacher development and literacy coordinator of her school district. She has expertise in working with students from culturally and linguistically diverse backgrounds, and her research examines literacy learning for emergent bilinguals, students who struggle with learning to read, and biliteracy development for Spanish speakers. She is lead author of the *Words Their Way with English Learners* and *Palabras a Su Paso* series as well as of *Literacy Instruction in Multilingual Classrooms* from Teachers College Press.

Carrie Rogers, PhD, is associate professor at Western Carolina University in the School of Teaching and Learning. She earned her doctorate after being a classroom teacher in Minneapolis for several years. Her research interests are practical leadership and teacher agency. Her areas of expertise are action research and curriculum development, with an emphasis on connecting the two while assisting teachers as they conduct research within their own classrooms to improve curriculum delivery and student learning.

Amy Frederick, PhD, is assistant professor at the University of Wisconsin – River Falls in the Teacher Education Department. She was an ELL teacher, professional developer, and literacy coach before earning her doctorate in literacy at the University of Minnesota. Her expertise is in teaching literacy with young emergent bilinguals and working with teachers in this area. She conducts professional development, presents at conferences, and authors curricular resources for teaching English learners.

Maggie Struck, MA, is a PhD candidate in literacy in the Department of Curriculum and Instruction at the University of Minnesota. She brings a history of community activism, youth work, and public elementary school teaching to her current academic work. Influenced by her dedication to both educational equity and building bridges between young people's literacy practices in community-based organizations and their literacy practices in school settings, her research focuses on young people's literacy practices in participatory learning cultures across these settings. She is interested in understanding how learning can enhance the social and academic futures of all students, specifically students who traditionally have been marginalized in public school settings.